Landscaping with Herbs

BEAUTIFY YOUR YARD AND GARDEN WITH EASY-CARE HERBS

Nancy J. Ondra

RODALE®

For Mom and Dad — thanks for your unfailing support!

 **RODALE**

**WE INSPIRE AND ENABLE PEOPLE TO IMPROVE
THEIR LIVES AND THE WORLD AROUND THEM**

Storey Books:
Editors: Gwen W. Steege and Jeanée Ledoux
Text designer: Eugenie Seidenberg Delaney
Text illustrator: All illustrations by Beverly Duncan, with the following exceptions: Sarah Brill, p. 17, 55, 70, 78, 83, 98, 100, 116; Judy Eliason, p. 36; Lavonne Francis, p. 50 and 86; Brigita Fuhrmann, p. 17 (top), 31 (top), 61 (bottom), 72, 76, 77, 85, 88, 94, 95, 96, 110, 119, 134, 147; Charles Joslin, p. 56, 74, 108, 121, 122, 124; Alison Kolesar, p. 111; and Louise Riotte, p. 84, 101, 102.
Production Assistant: Jennifer Jepson Smith
Indexer: Susan Olason, Indexes & Knowledge Maps

Rodale Organic Gardening Books:
Managing Editor: Fern Marshall Bradley
Editor: Karen Costello Soltys
Executive Creative Director: Christin Gangi
Art Director/Cover Designer: Patricia Field
Studio Manager: Leslie Keefe
Manufacturing Manager: Mark Krahforst

We're always happy to hear from you. For questions or comments concerning the editorial content of this book, please write to:
Rodale Book Readers' Service
33 East Minor Street
Emmaus, PA 18098

Look for other Rodale books wherever books are sold. Or call us at (800) 848-4735.

For more information about Rodale Organic Gardening magazine and books, visit us at
www.organicgardening.com

Library of Congress Cataloging-in-Publication Data

Ondra, Nancy J.
    Landscaping with herbs : beautify your yard and garden with easy-care
herbs / Nancy J. Ondra.
        p.   cm. — (Rodale's essential herbal handbooks)
    Includes bibliographical references (p.) and index.
    ISBN 0–87596–857–0 (hardcover)
    ISBN 0–87596–858–9 (pbk.)
    1. Herb gardening. 2. Landscape gardening. 3. Herbs. I. Title. II. Series.
SB351.H5 O53 2000
635.9'68—dc21   99–050813

Distributed in the book trade by St. Martin's Press
Printed in the United States of America
2 4 6 8 10 9 7 5 3 1   hardcover
2 4 6 8 10 9 7 5 3   papercover

Contents

CHAPTER 1

HERBS, HERBS

Everywhere!

Sooner or later, just about every gardener gets the surge to grow herbs. And when you start looking through the hundreds of books and magazines on the subject, you'll find lots of information on creating and caring for herb gardens. These versatile plants have lots to offer all parts of your landscape, from flower beds and borders to pots and planters. Some produce beautiful flowers, while others contribute fragrant foliage, and all can add a touch of history and practicality to any planting.

Happily, mingling herbs with annuals, perennials, shrubs, and other plantings doesn't take a special touch, just a knowledge of basic good gardening. Before we get into the specific herbs and how to grow them, let's explore some of the many ways you can work herbs into your existing landscape or create new herb-enhanced plantings.

EXPLORING YOUR HERBAL OPTIONS

Traditional herb gardens are generally sited in open, full-sun sites, but you don't need a flat field to grow these versatile plants. Look around your existing landscape, and what do you see: shady spots, flower beds, slopes, a vegetable garden, a deck or patio? You can find herbs to fit all of these sites and more!

HERBS FOR FLOWERS AND FRAGRANCE

Don't buy the rumor that herbs are plain green and boring. These plants are pretty as well as practical. Even among those that mostly produce leaves, you can find herbs in a wide range of foliage colors, including all shades of green, blue-gray, purple, silver, gold, and red-brown. And don't forget all of the great variegated herbs, with leaves that are splashed, spotted, streaked, or dotted with contrasting colors.

Herbs are no slouches in the flower department, either. In fact, many of the most popular flowering perennials, including catmints (*Nepeta* species), lady's mantle *(Alchemilla mollis)*, purple coneflower *(Echinacea purpurea)*, and yarrows (*Achillea* species), have long been prized by herb gardeners for their healing properties.

Fragrance, of course, is another reason to include herbs in every garden. Scented flowers are lovely, but there's something special about the way herbs wait until you touch them to release their aromas. They give you a reason to wander farther into the garden, to see the plants up close and enjoy the way they feel as well as the way they look.

Herbs are more than just pretty faces! Give them a gentle rub and they'll share their enticing aromas.

HERBS IN DIFFICULT SITES

While a wide variety of herbs grow just fine in sun and average garden soil, others are well adapted to out-of-the-ordinary conditions. Trees and shrubs casting summer shade? No problem at all —

mints (*Mentha* species) and sweet woodruff *(Galium odoratum)* are just two of the shade-tolerant herbs. Hot, dry slopes where grass won't grow? Don't sweat it — try artemisias (*Artemisia* species), thymes (*Thymus* species), and a variety of other herbs that appreciate those harsh conditions.

HERBS IN UNEXPECTED PLACES

Get your herbal garden started by incorporating herbs into your existing flower beds and borders. Mix ornamental herbs like lady's mantle and catmints with more traditional annuals and perennials and then go one step further by using the herbs as edging plants. Expand your herbal plantings by siting them along paths and walkways. Let them spill onto the paving for a casual look or trim them into low hedges for a more formal feel. Turn tough-to-mow sites into easy-care areas by replacing the grass with a carpet of low-growing and low-maintenance herbs.

Of course, you don't want to forget the vegetable garden! Plant your favorite culinary herbs such as basil, parsley, or dill among your vegetable crops for one-stop harvesting. And don't let that deck or patio go unplanted, either: Sitting areas are excellent places for container herb gardens. You can even incorporate herbs into hanging baskets and window boxes. Once you get started with herbal landscaping, the possibilities are endless!

Place a pot of herbs by your favorite deck chair so you can get up-close-and-personal with these rewarding and easy-to-grow plants.

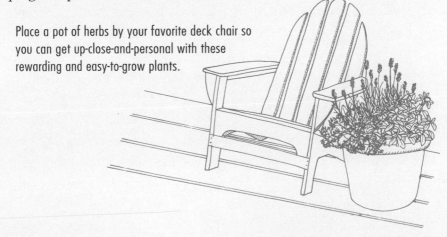

ADDING HERBS TO BEDS AND BORDERS

Flower beds and borders are perfect places to start adding herbs to your landscape. With their wide range of heights and habits, herbs can fit into any part of any planting. Here are some specific ways to integrate herbs into your yard and garden.

BEAUTIFUL BLOOMS

While herbs have a reputation for being plain and practical, many of them can hold their own against traditional flower-garden residents. From creeping carpets of thyme to towering clumps of angelica *(Angelica archangelica),* these lovely plants make a perfect complement to standard annuals and perennials.

Low-growing herbs for edging. For the front of the border, you can choose from a variety of low-growing herbs. For instance, the sunny-colored, daisylike flowers of calendulas *(Calendula officinalis)* and the bright-hued blooms of nasturtiums *(Tropaeolum majus)* are excellent choices for quick color. These annuals are also great for tucking into gaps while you're waiting for perennial plantings to fill in.

For a more permanent edging effect, consider a row of pink- or white-flowered bushy thymes. The bees will love you for it! And don't forget the frothy yellowish flowers of lady's mantle or the sweet purple-blue blooms of catmints. These front-of-the-border standbys have been so popular for so long that you'll often see them treated as traditional perennials rather than as herbs — a perfect example of how these versatile plants work as well in the landscape as they do in the herb garden.

Medium-height herbs for the middle of a border. Medium-sized herbs that work well midborder may also be just the right scale for the back of a small bed. What would summer be without the red blooms of bee balms (*Monarda* species), the bright yellow flowers of yarrows, or the rosy pink daisies of purple coneflower? Other good choices for midborder include oreganos *(Origanum vulgare),* fever-few *(Tanacetum parthenium),* and, of course, the lovely lavenders (*Lavandula* species).

Tall herbs for the background. Not to be overlooked, taller herbs offer fabulous flowers for the back of a border. Anise hyssops (*Agastache* species) produce handsome waist-high clumps of spiky purple blooms month after month, while yellow-flowered fennel (*Foeniculum vulgare)* and mulleins (*Verbascum* species) can easily reach eye level or even higher.

FABULOUS FOLIAGE

Too many gardeners think of foliage as simply a filler around flowers. My personal motto is "Flowers are fleeting, but foliage is forever." I like my gardens to look good from early spring through fall, and there aren't too many plants that can offer flower color that long. For season-long interest, foliage is the key.

Leaves come in an amazing range of greens, but that's just the beginning. Herbs offer some of the most spectacular silvery foliage, notably in the artemisias, lavenders, and santolinas (*Santolina* species). And when you start investigating the more unusual selections, you'll find a whole range of hues, from the chocolate-brown leaves of bronze fennel (*Foeniculum vulgare* 'Purpureum') to the bright yellow foliage of golden feverfew (*Tanacetum parthenium* 'Aureum'). Variegated foliage also abounds in herbs, from the white-edged leaves of pineapple mint (*Mentha suaveolens* 'Variegata') to the lovely yellow-and-green blending on golden sage (*Salvia officinalis* 'Icterina'). When you choose a variety of herbs with colorful foliage for a bed or border, you're guaranteed a great show from spring to frost.

If you're looking for an herb that can't be missed, consider a clump of angelica. Its greenish white flowers bloom atop stems that can easily reach 6 feet or higher!

GROWING HERBS AS GROUND COVERS

If you need a ground cover for your garden, don't think you're stuck with uninspiring sheets of pachysandra, periwinkle, or ivy. With so many great low-growing herbs to choose from, you can have a gorgeous ground cover that offers beautiful flowers and fabulous fragrance to boot!

HERBS UNDER TREES

Growing grass under trees can be a real maintenance headache. Lawn turf is often sparse due to the shady conditions, so weeds quickly fill in, and mowing over exposed tree roots is bad for both your mower and your tree. Planting a carpet of creeping herbs can turn a difficult spot into a handsome, easy-care landscape feature.

The first steps to creating an herbal ground cover are removing any existing grass and weeds and then preparing the soil. Planting under trees is a bit of a challenge, since you can't just go in with a rotary tiller and quickly loosen the earth. Trees produce many surface roots that play an important role in seeking out water and nutrients, and damaging them can seriously injure your tree. Dumping loose topsoil on the soil surface can also be a problem, since it might smother and kill those important feeder roots. To get around these problems, I prefer to start with small plants and dig individual planting pockets for each one. That minimizes disturbance to the tree, and I find that small plants often settle in and spread more quickly than larger plants. For tips on using this technique, turn to Shady Strategies on page 42.

Once your herbs have filled in and covered the site, trim them two or three times during the growing season to keep them tidy and encourage low, bushy growth. Use a string trimmer, or even garden shears if you have a small patch, to minimize damage to the plant crowns. Lightly rake off the trimmings so they don't smother the plants. Also rake off any dropped tree leaves in fall, and pull out any weeds that pop up throughout the growing season. Other than that, your herbal lawn needs little other care.

Great Ground Cover Herbs

Check out these low-growing herbs to cover a bare spot in your garden.

Roman chamomile *(Chamaemelum nobile)*. With its soft carpet of sweet-scented foliage and small white daisies, chamomile is cheerful and inviting in sunny, well-drained sites.

Pennyroyal *(Mentha pulegium)*. All mints spread quickly in rich, evenly moist soil, but pennyroyal is an especially good choice for its ground-hugging habit and shade tolerance.

Common oregano *(Origanum vulgare)*. It's tough and adaptable, and it spreads at a moderate pace in sun to partial shade. Shear the stems back to 2 to 3 inches just as the flowers open to encourage lower, bushy growth.

Sweet woodruff *(Galium odoratum)*. A popular choice for shady sites, this delicate-looking but sturdy herb can spread quickly.

Thymes. Creeping thyme *(Thymus praecox* subspecies *arcticus)* and woolly thyme (*T. praecox* subspecies *arcticus* 'Lanuginosus') are particularly good choices for sunny sites, as they seldom reach even a few inches tall.

HERBAL TURF

Low-growing herbs make super ground covers for sunny sites as well. In fact, you can even use them to replace turfgrass. They won't stand up to soccer games or romping dogs, but they do make great low-maintenance grass alternatives in side yards and other low-traffic sites.

Roman chamomile is a favorite for herbal lawns, since it can take a light amount of foot traffic and it responds to occasional mowing by producing more spreading growth. Ground-hugging thymes are another popular choice, since they don't need trimming at all.

Starting an herbal lawn is pretty much the same as starting any other lawn when it comes to preparing the soil. While you can establish small areas from direct-sown seed, you'll get much faster results by starting with small plants spaced 4 to 6 inches apart.

Even with herbs that can tolerate light foot traffic, it's a good idea to add a few stepping-stones through your herbal lawn so you don't have to tread directly on the plants.

Enjoying Herbs as Edgings

For centuries, gardeners have enjoyed planting low-growing herbs along paths, where they could appreciate the pretty flowers and inhale the sweet scents as they brushed by the foliage. But don't overlook the value of taller herbs: They make super growing-season screens and barriers, and they offer the same floral and foliage benefits!

HERBAL HEDGES

Compact, bushy, and mounding herbs are excellent for creating low hedges for all kinds of edges: skirting steps, surrounding patios, and flanking paths and walkways. Low herbal hedges also look great enclosing flower beds and borders.

Need a taller planting to divide a lawn area, screen off the vegetable garden or compost bins, or block an unsightly view? Grow a row of tall herbs, such as angelicas, anise hyssops, fennel, rue *(Ruta graveolens),* or southernwood *(Artemisia abrotanum).* Set the plants close together — 2 feet apart for angelicas and 12 to 18 inches apart for the others — and these herbs will produce a dense barrier that serves as an effective screen through most of the growing season.

Depending on your tastes, herbal hedges can be formal or informal. Many herbs tolerate regular trimming, so you can prune them into rectangles or other shapes. Germander *(Teucrium chamaedrys),* hyssop *(Hyssopus officinalis),* lavenders, and santolinas are traditional favorites for trimmed herbal hedges. Their small leaves and bushy habits produce tidy, dense edgings. Back in Elizabethan times, gardeners often used one or more low herb hedges to outline geometric patterns called "knot gardens"; you can see re-creations of these in some places today. For more information on knot gardens, see Creating Herbal Theme Gardens on page 14.

Germander

Formal hedges look best if you keep them about 1 foot tall. This requires a hard pruning in spring (cut them back by one-third to one-half), then regular clipping every two to three weeks from late May to early July to keep them looking regular and neat.

For more casual lawns, informal herbal hedges look good too, and they're a lot less work to maintain. Just give them a light trimming, if needed, in midspring to shape them up a bit, and they'll produce a tidy but more casual-looking edging.

A lavender-lined path not only looks terrific but also sends up a delicious scent whenever you brush by it.

Best Herbs for Edges

Try these bushy beauties when you want to create an herbal edging along a path or walkway.

Catmint. Gray-green foliage and purple-blue blooms; takes light shearing but looks best left in its natural mounded form.

Germander. Shiny green foliage; tolerates hard trimming.

Hyssop. Narrow green leaves; withstands hard pruning.

Lavender. Fragrant silvery foliage; responds well to clipping.

Santolina. Aromatic silvery or green foliage; looks best with regular pruning (about once every three weeks).

Thyme. Fragrant foliage and flowers; stays tidy even without trimming.

HERBS ALONG CURBS

One common landscape challenge is that strip of grass left between a sidewalk and a street curb. Consider replacing that high-maintenance band of grass with a more interesting mix of low- to medium-height, heat-tolerant herbs. Good choices include silvery-leaved artemisias; aromatic lavenders, oreganos, santolinas, and thymes; blue-leaved rue; and colorful yarrows.

Before you plant, though, it's smart to check your local zoning laws or other land-use restrictions; there may be rules about the heights and kinds of plants you are allowed to grow in that strip.

GROWING HERBS IN CONTAINERS

When you're ready for something besides geraniums and vinca as your container plantings, consider herbs. Pots, planters, and window boxes are a particularly good way to enjoy low-growing, aromatic herbs such as thymes, since they're within easy reach for a rub between your fingers or even right at nose level for convenient sniffing.

Containers also let you grow herbs in spots where you can't have an in-ground garden, such as on a deck or terrace. In fact, I grow most of my culinary herbs in a collection of containers out by my sidewalk, since that's the sunniest spot I have. Using a variety of pots and planters lets me grow all the herbs I can use — and they look great, too!

POTS VERSUS PLANTERS

Herbs can adapt equally well to life in individual pots or grouped in larger planters. Growing each herb in its own pot gives you lots of flexibility, since you can easily move them to their preferred growing conditions or rearrange your container displays. Pots also are an excellent way to control mints and other herbs that spread quickly and smother close companions. On the downside, individual pots can dry out quickly, so you'll have to pay close attention to watering, dowsing them at least once a day and sometimes even twice a day during hot, dry spells. (This is especially true for herbs in window boxes and hanging baskets, which are more exposed to drying winds.)

Since larger planters hold a greater volume of growing medium, they can support several plants, and they need less frequent watering. On the other hand, planters can be very heavy and difficult to move. You need to decide where you want them and plan to leave them there, or else set them on wheeled platforms *before* you fill them with potting soil.

CONTAINER CONSIDERATIONS

You'll hear a lot of debate about the best material for herb containers, but it really depends on your individual conditions. Clay pots are a traditional favorite; they look good but tend to dry out quickly. I like to use them for herbs that definitely don't like soggy soil, such as oreganos, rosemary *(Rosmarinus officinalis)*, and thymes. I prefer plastic or fiberglass pots for herbs that like to be evenly moist, including basils *(Ocimum* species), mints, and sorrels *(Rumex* species), especially if they are in full-sun sites. If even plastic pots need to be watered more than once daily, place a saucer under each and fill it once a day to provide a steady water source for the roots.

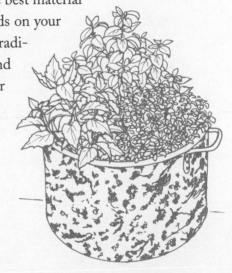

It's fun to experiment with unusual containers, such as old boots, spatterware canning pots, and other found objects. Just make sure that you add some kind of drainage holes if they are lacking.

SOIL AND NOURISHMENT NEEDS

Don't be tempted to fill any container with straight garden soil. Regular watering will quickly compact it into a tight mass that roots can't penetrate. It's easiest to start with a commercially available growing medium from your local home and garden center or nursery. I've had good results using an all-purpose mix for potting all of my container herbs.

Looking for something different to perk up your container plantings? Try some of these partnerships:

Golden feverfew and red leaf lettuce (*Tanacetum parthenium* 'Aureum' and 'Merlot' lettuce). Great in window boxes

Spanish lavender and heliotrope (*Lavandula stoechas* and *Heliotropium arborescens*). A fragrant silver-and-purple pairing

Peppermint geranium and white impatiens (*Pelargonium tomentosum* and *Impatiens* species). A cool green-and-white grouping for shade

Bush basil and dwarf cherry tomato (*Ocimum basilicum* 'Minimum' and 'Birdie Mix' for the tomato). Pretty and edible

Besides watering, container gardens need regular fertilizing to look their best. Fertilize once every two to three weeks by watering with diluted fish emulsion, seaweed extract, or a commercial organic liquid fertilizer.

MIXING HERBS AND VEGETABLES

Growing herbs in your vegetable garden is certainly a smart idea. What could be easier than having your dinner fixings and seasonings all in one spot? As a plus, herbs can be a big help to your vegetables, both by discouraging pests and by attracting pollinators and other beneficial insects for better yields.

HERBS HELPING VEGETABLES

The idea of plants helping each other isn't a new one. Gardeners have been enjoying its benefits for hundreds of years. You'll often hear this system of planned plant partnerships called "companion planting."

Of the many claims for ways herbs can benefit vegetables, some are part folklore while others are scientifically proven. Some gardeners, for instance, believe herb odors can mask or hide a crop from pests. Catnip *(Nepeta cataria)* and other mints, for instance, are supposed to repel aphids and cabbage pests, while sweet basil *(Ocimum basilicum)* is said to repel hornworms from tomatoes. Other herbs actually attract pests away from other plants. Nasturtiums, for

Great-Tasting Groupings

Make dinner preparation a snap by planting your favorite herb-and-vegetable combinations together. Here are a few tasty pairings to try:

Basil and tomatoes. These two are a perfect pairing! Besides tasting great, basils can help protect your tomatoes from hornworms.

Chives and potatoes. What would a baked potato be without a dab of sour cream and a scattering of chives? The mild onion flavor also tastes terrific with fried or boiled potatoes.

Dill and carrots. The feathery foliage of dill adds a nice touch to cooked carrots, and these partners are also tasty raw in green salads.

Oregano and eggplant. These staples of Italian cuisine are a natural partnership. Combine them with basil, peppers, and zucchini, and you have months' worth of dinner ingredients!

Thyme and green beans. Thyme's flavorful foliage blends well with most vegetables, but it's especially tasty with beans. Experiment with different types of thyme to find your favorite combinations.

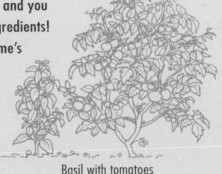

Basil with tomatoes

Thyme with green beans

Dill with carrots

instance, are very popular with aphids, so the pests will attack these plants and pass by others.

Two definite benefits herbs can provide are food and shelter for beneficial insects. Some of these insects, such as bees and syrphid flies, are important pollinators for your crops. Bee balms are some of the most well-known choices, but anise hyssops, catmints, lemon balm *(Melissa officinalis)*, oreganos, and thymes are all very popular with bees. Other beneficials eat pest insects during part or all of their life cycles. When their bodies are developing, or when pests are lacking, beneficials rely on pollen and nectar for proteins and sugar. Herbs with small but abundant blooms, including angelica, dill, fennel, and yarrows, are excellent food sources for beneficials. A healthy population of beneficial insects is one of the best ways to keep your vegetables pest-free and productive.

CREATING HERBAL THEME GARDENS

Some people collect pottery, others like artwork. Gardeners collect plants! A fun way to direct your collecting is creating theme gardens to showcase your special interests. If you have a small garden, choosing one theme can help unify the design, even if you grow a wide variety of plants. In a larger garden, you can create a number of different theme plantings in which to group your favorite herbs.

Besides enjoying the plants themselves, you'll get other benefits from creating theme gardens. For instance, you have the fun of choosing a theme and then researching to find out which plants are appropriate. Once you start developing a plant list (and that's an ongoing process), you'll enjoy searching out some of the more unusual selections to complete your collection.

HISTORICAL THEME GARDENS

Choosing a certain time period is a particularly fascinating way to guide your collecting endeavors. Some people like to collect herbs that were mentioned in the Bible, such as rue, or those related to saints and angels, such as angelica and lady's mantle. Others enjoy gathering plants around a medieval theme, which often means growing plants that have a practical use, such as food, flavoring, dyes, or medicine. Other options are a Shakespearean planting or a seventeenth- or eighteenth-century theme garden.

To Garden or Knot?

"Knot gardens" — geometric patterns outlined with low hedges — were a popular landscape feature in Elizabethan times. Designed mainly to be viewed from above, these handsome but high-maintenance plantings were commonly composed of tightly clipped herbs, including germander, hyssop, and lavenders. Using a combination of silver- and green-leaved herbs added extra interest to the patterns, as did using different colors of gravel to fill the spaces between the hedges.

One drawback of knot gardens is that even a relatively simple pattern outlined with 1-foot-tall hedges can take up a lot of room. If you like the idea of creating a knot garden but have limited space, consider using a variety of bushy thymes to outline your pattern. These lower-growing herbs come in a range of colors, and they tolerate frequent trimming. Best of all, you'll enjoy the aroma when you clip them!

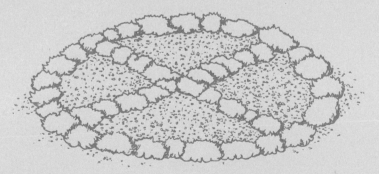

To create a miniature knot garden, plant thyme hedges and clip them to about 4 inches tall. Regular shearing with hedge trimmers — every three weeks or so — will keep the hedges neat so the pattern stays visible.

PLANTS WITH A PURPOSE

Another way to organize your plantings is by grouping herbs and other plants by their uses. You might choose a medicinal garden, a tea garden, or a dye garden, depending on your interests. If you are into crafts, a cut-flower or dried-flower garden could be a good choice. While these theme gardens are certainly practical, you don't have to actually *use* the plants for their intended purpose; you could just have fun learning how and why they are useful.

For More Inspiration

One of my favorite herbal memories is a trip friends and I took to Caprilands Herb Farm in Coventry, Connecticut, in the late 1980s. Caprilands's creator, Adele Grenier Simmons, had fashioned a wonderland of herbal theme gardens, from the Fragrance Garden and Garden Tinctoria (plants that were used for dyes) to the Shakespeare Garden, Eighteenth-Century Garden, and Victorian Garden. We also saw gardens arranged by plant groupings, including the Thyme Terrace and Geranium Garden, as well as color groupings based on blue, yellow, or silver plants.

While this great lady has since passed away, the gardens are still cared for and open to the public. If you aren't lucky enough to visit in person, you can check out the gardens on the World Wide Web (see Herbal Resources on page 149). I also highly recommend reading Ms. Simmons's books (available through the Web site), especially *A Garden Walk,* which is a virtual tour through the amazing array of theme gardens at Caprilands.

MAKING GREAT COMBINATIONS

No doubt about it — good gardening starts with choosing the right plants for each site. If an herb isn't suited to the growing conditions you have to offer, it won't thrive, and no amount of careful design planning is going to work. But beyond that, there are several points to consider when putting plants together.

CHOOSE A COLOR THEME

If you haven't already selected a particular theme (such as a butterfly garden or a certain time period), color is a super starting point for creating plant combinations. You don't have to limit yourself to just one color — all white flowers, for instance; choosing two or three colors can work just as well. In my garden, I keep the bright yellows, oranges, and reds together in one area, while the pale yellows, pinks, and blues get their own border in another spot. This kind of overall grouping definitely helps when you're wandering around your yard with a trowel and yet another new plant to tuck in. If you find it a spot among like-colored companions, there's a good chance it will look like it always belonged there!

START WITH FOLIAGE

I admire photographs of gardens filled with lovely flower combinations, but I always wonder what those same gardens look like a week or month later, when the flowers are finished. On a large property, you can get away with that, since you have the room to create separate gardens that look good in different seasons. But when you're working with limited space, you want your whole garden to look its best for the longest possible time. The way to do that is to include lots of plants with interesting foliage.

Fennel

What makes foliage interesting? Well, it could have an unusual shape or texture: ferny or feathery, such as fennel; narrow and needlelike, such as rosemary; or big and fuzzy, such as mulleins. Another aspect of foliage interest comes from the "anything-but-green" group: plants that offer silvery, gray, blue, yellow, brown, purple, or variegated leaves. Herbs as a group seem especially generous in providing colored-foliage options for adventurous gardeners. Including these plants in your garden will go a long way toward creating many-hued, all-season interest.

Mullein

Problem-Solving with Herbs

Maybe you have a hot, sunny slope that's a hassle to mow, a low spot where water puddles after a rain, or a shady site where most plants just don't thrive. Fortunately, there's at least one herb to fit just about any problem area.

Heat-Tolerant Herbs

Looking for plants that can tolerate a hot, sunny spot, such as a slope or a bed along a street or driveway? Here are some suggestions.

Artemisias. These silvery-leaved beauties are great for adding height and attractive foliage to a hot site.

Catmints. Purple-blue flowers accent these gray-green mounds for months.

Lavenders. Full sun and excellent drainage are musts for success with these beloved herbs.

Santolinas. Sunny yellow flowers dot tight mounds of silvery or bright green foliage.

Thymes. Both bushy and creeping types offer aromatic foliage and tiny but numerous blooms.

Herbs for Wet Spots

While few herbs will thrive in waterlogged soil, some can tolerate an evenly moist or even an occasionally soggy site.

Angelicas. These high-reaching herbs make an impact in damp-soil sites.

Bee balms. Evenly moist soil is ideal for keeping most bee balms healthy; they'll spread quickly here, though!

Mints. These creeping herbs also travel rapidly in moist soil, providing quick cover.

Sweet woodruff. It looks delicate, but this lovely herb will form a dense, weed-suppressing ground cover.

Shade-Adapted Herbs

Shady spots are a real landscape challenge, but they can also be beautiful garden features if you fill them with carefully chosen plants. Here are some herbs that can adapt to sites with filtered sunlight for most of the day, or at least 2 hours of direct sun.

Angelicas. Light shade is ideal for these large herbs, especially in hot-summer climates.

Lemon balm *(Melissa officinalis)*. Plant these mounded herbs along a woodland path and enjoy their fresh citrus scent as you brush by the foliage.

Mints. Mowing mints just before bloom will help them produce a dense, scented carpet in shady spots.

Oregano, common. Most oreganos prefer full sun, but common oregano can get by in partial shade. 'Aureum' is especially nice.

Parsley. These ferny, bright green mounds make excellent edgings or fillers in shady gardens.

Sweet woodruff. A woodland native, sweet woodruff is a natural choice for covering the ground under trees and shrubs.

THINK IN THREES AND FOURS

While starting a new garden with a carefully thought-out plan is a smart way to go, I must admit that I'm seldom that organized. When I have some open ground and a bunch of herbs that need homes, I want to plant, not plan! You can easily come up with effective combinations "on the fly" if you break your collection down into groups of three or four plants.

I like to start with a plant that has colorful leaves, then choose two or three companions that include those colors in their leaves and/or flowers. In a shady spot, for instance, you might start with a white-and-green–leaved hosta, then add sweet woodruff for its curiously whorled green leaves and white spring flowers. Toss in some white-flowered impatiens, and you have a grouping that looks good until frost. A sunny-site combination might start with golden sage and then add lower-growing golden oregano and the gray-green leaves and greenish yellow flowers of lady's mantle. Use these simple combinations as building blocks, and in no time you'll have a great-looking garden!

Lovely Leaves

While herbs come in a lovely range of green hues, you can choose from many other foliage colors. Here are a few of my favorites:

Blue or blue-gray. Rue and catmints

Brown or purple. Purple basils (such as 'Purple Ruffles' and 'Red Rubin'), purple sage (*Salvia officinalis* 'Purpureum'), bronze fennel

Silver. Artemisias, lavenders, lavender cotton (*Santolina chamaecyparissus*)

Yellow. Golden feverfew, golden oregano, golden lemon balm

Yellow-and-green. Golden sage and variegated lemon thyme (*Thymus x citriodorus* 'Aureus')

White-and-green or white-and-blue. Pineapple mint and variegated rue (*Ruta graveolens* 'Variegata')

CHAPTER 2

A GALLERY
OF HERBAL
Landscapes

With so many beautiful herbs to choose from and so many great combinations possible, you might wonder where to start in planning a garden. In this chapter, you'll find simple designs for eight different gardens to help get you going with your new herbal landscape. I've included gardens for a variety of sites and situations. Choose one, or several, that capture your imagination.

While you could certainly plant these plans as is, I encourage you to use them as inspiration for creating your own herb-based garden designs. Don't worry if you can't find the particular species or cultivars that are listed in a certain design. Just work with whatever herbs you can find at first and then fine-tune the planting later as you are able to find sources for more unusual herbs.

A HUMMINGBIRD AND BUTTERFLY GARDEN

Hummingbirds and butterflies occasionally visit almost any landscape, but if you want to improve your odds of attracting these beautiful creatures, consider creating a garden just for them. It's easy to do: Just choose a sunny spot, plant a selection of suitable flowers and herbs, and wait for the wildlife to visit!

What is it that makes some plants more attractive than others? Sometimes it's the food they supply. Both butterflies and hummingbirds are on the lookout for plants that can provide ample quantities of nectar. Hummingbirds are particularly fond of plants with showy red, tubular flowers, such as bee balms and sages. Butterflies appreciate these too, but they also enjoy clusters of many tiny flowers, such as the centers of daisylike German chamomile *(Matricaria recutita)* blooms or the small flowers of dill, fennel, mints, lavenders, oreganos, thymes, and yarrows.

Butterflies are also seeking good egg-laying spots — plants that can provide the food their caterpillars will need. Black swallowtails, for instance, will frequent your parsley patch to lay eggs, which later produce the distinctive bright-green-and-black-banded caterpillars.

When you plan a hummingbird and butterfly garden, you'll want to keep some special considerations in mind. First of all, when you attract butterflies, they in turn may lay eggs, and the resulting caterpillars will feed on your plants. For that reason, you may choose to site this kind of garden in a somewhat out-of-the-way spot, so the chewed leaves aren't easily visible. On the other hand, you do want to be able to see the hummingbirds and butterflies, so consider siting the garden near a side window or placing a bench nearby for easy viewing. And while it's best to minimize chemical use in any garden, it's especially important to avoid spraying in this type of planting. You don't want to kill off the very creatures you are trying to attract!

German chamomile

Hummingbird and Butterfly Garden

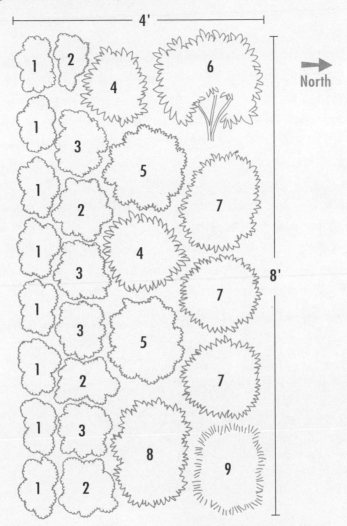

PLANT LIST

1. Parsley, 8*
2. Variegated lemon thyme (*Thymus* x *citriodorus* 'Aureus'), 4
3. Golden oregano (*Origanum vulgare* 'Aureum'), 4
4. Purple coneflower (*Echinacea purpurea*), 2
5. 'Terra Cotta' yarrow (*Achillea millefolium* 'Terra Cotta'), 2
6. 'Pink Delight' butterfly bush (*Buddleia davidii* 'Pink Delight'), 1
7. Anise hyssop (*Agastache foeniculum*), 3
8. 'Marshall's Delight' bee balm (*Monarda* 'Marshall's Delight'), 1
9. Bronze fennel (*Foeniculum vulgare* 'Purpureum'), 1

*The number after the botanical name indicates the number of plants needed.

Besides choosing plants they like, you can do some other things to make your landscape a haven for hummingbirds and butterflies. Here are two easy ideas to try:

Hang a hummingbird feeder. Buy an inexpensive plastic nectar feeder, one with those gaudy red parts that attract the birds' attention. Fill it with instant nectar mix (available at wild bird supply stores) or with sugar water (add 1 part sugar to 4 parts boiling water, then let mixture cool before filling the feeder). Change the sweet solution and clean the feeder every few days to keep the liquid fresh.

Make a mud puddle. Butterflies get thirsty, too, so they need a source of water. You'll often see them congregating around mud puddles. If you have a spot to create one for them, they'll appreciate it. If that isn't an option, fill a shallow tray with rocks and water to create a "bug bath."

Add just enough water to your bug bath to partially cover the rocks, so the butterflies (and other insects) can land on the islands and drink without falling in.

CUSTOMIZING THIS DESIGN

In addition to the plants recommended in this design, hummingbirds and butterflies have many other favorites. Here are some additional ideas:

Herbal extravaganza. If you want to expand this planting with more herbs that appeal to butterflies and hummingbirds, consider any or all of the following: angelicas, calendula, catmints, both Roman and German chamomile, chives, dill, feverfew, hyssop, lavenders, mints, sages, and scented geraniums.

Grow up. Hummingbirds love the colorful blooms of many annual and perennial vines, including Chilean glory flower *(Eccremocarpus scaber)*, cardinal climber *(Ipomoea × multifida)*, cypress vine *(I. quamoclit)*, and honeysuckles *(Lonicera* species).

While eastern gardeners see only one hummingbird species (the ruby-throated) several other species grace western gardens. Westerners also have many beautiful native plants to attract hummingbirds — desert willow *(Chilopsis linearis)*, ocotillo *(Fouquieria splendens)*, and California fuchsia *(Zauschneria californica)*, just to name a few.

PROBLEM PREVENTION

This garden is designed to attract insects, so don't be surprised to see a few holes in some leaves or a couple of chewed parsley stems. Overall, though, pest damage should be minimal, since the same flowers that draw in butterflies also attract a wide variety of beneficial insects. If you do spot some pests, squash them with your fingers, trim them off with pruning shears, or knock them off the plants with a strong spray of water. Avoid using soap sprays or stronger chemicals.

None of these plants are particularly prone to disease problems, as long as you grow them in full sun and average, well-drained soil. Bee balms are notoriously susceptible to powdery mildew, a fungal disease that produces dusty gray patches on leaves, stems, and buds. Seriously affected plants tend to drop their lower leaves. For this garden, though, I've recommended the pink-flowered bee balm cultivar 'Marshall's Delight'. This mildew-resistant selection performs well in my garden, showing barely any mildew damage even when other bee balms are covered with mildew. If you prefer red flowers, consider 'Jacob Cline'; it, too, is very mildew resistant and bears huge blooms that my resident hummingbird just loves!

CARE THROUGH THE SEASONS

This garden includes a collection of easy-care, dependable herbs, so you can get it started pretty much any time the plants are available. Early to midspring and late summer to early fall are ideal planting times for most of the perennials, because temperatures are moderate and rainfall is usually more dependable, but even summer planting can work if you are willing and able to water regularly. In Zones 4 to 6, plant the butterfly bush in fall or spring; south of Zone 6, set it out in fall or winter.

Early to midspring. If you set out your plants in spring, water them thoroughly and then apply a 2-inch layer of an organic mulch, such as chopped leaves or shredded bark. Keep a 2- to 4-inch-wide mulch-free zone around the base of each plant. If rain is lacking, check the soil under the mulch and water when the top inch or two is dry.

Spring is also a good time to tidy up established gardens. Remove conifer branches or other winter mulch and clean up any debris that has collected over the months. Cut remaining top growth (except for the butterfly bush) to just above the ground.

If your garden is already established, you may find that last year's parsley plants survived the winter, and you might be tempted to leave them for another season. But parsley is a biennial, which means that the plants will produce flowers, set seed, and die early in their second year. Yes, they will still add color to your garden, and the flowers will attract some butterflies and beneficial insects, but you'll lose that nice mounding effect that makes parsley such an excellent edging plant. It's best to replace your parsley border every year by setting out seedlings along the front edge of the garden in the spring.

Scatter a ½-inch layer of compost and, if needed, a few handfuls of a balanced organic fertilizer over the soil every spring to provide a steady supply of nutrients for good growth.

Midspring to midsummer. During dry spells, water new plantings as needed to keep the soil evenly moist. Established herbs can tolerate dry conditions, so there's no need to water them unless rainfall is lacking and the top 2 or 3 inches of soil are dry under the mulch. Pull out any weeds that pop up through the mulch and add more mulch if needed to maintain a 1- to 2-inch layer.

Midsummer to midfall. To keep your plants looking their best and minimize self-sowing, remove spent flowers regularly. On anise hyssop, bee balm, butterfly bush, fennel, and purple coneflower, trim the flowers off just above the uppermost leaf or leaf pair. Cut off the spent yarrow flowers at the base of the plant. That's the only care this garden will need, other than to water, weed, and add mulch if necessary.

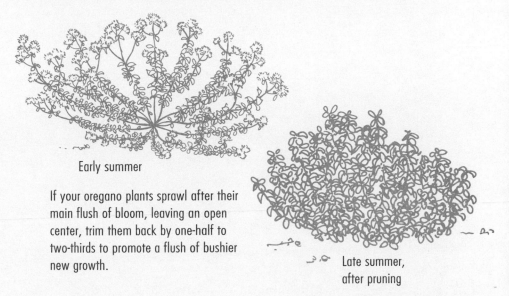

Early summer

If your oregano plants sprawl after their main flush of bloom, leaving an open center, trim them back by one-half to two-thirds to promote a flush of bushier new growth.

Late summer, after pruning

Midfall through winter. If you set out hummingbird and butterfly plants in fall, water them thoroughly after planting but hold off on the organic mulch for a bit. Once the soil is frozen, new plantings benefit from a lightweight winter mulch, such as evergreen branches or a few inches of loose straw. Established gardens also benefit from a protective winter mulch, especially north of Zone 6.

If you don't apply a winter mulch, check the garden every week or two (especially after a warm spell) to make sure the freezing and thawing isn't pushing any of your plants out of the soil. If you do see frost-heaved plants, cover the exposed roots with mulch or soil to keep them from drying out. In early spring, dig up the heaved plants and reset them at the proper planting depth.

To keep your butterfly bush vigorous and free-blooming, prune it in winter, cutting one-third of the oldest stems to the ground each year to leave an open, arching framework. Or, if you'd prefer a bushier, more compact plant, cut all of the stems right at ground level.

A Rock Wall Garden

Sloping sites can be a real challenge in the landscape. It's tough to get plants growing there, since water runs right off the steep surface, making it hard for young roots to get established. One solution is to grow turfgrass, but even if this is possible, then you're stuck with a difficult or even dangerous mowing job. Another way to handle these troublesome sites is to install one or more low walls to break up the slope and create flat planting areas known as terraces.

Walls and terraces provide perfect growing conditions for a wide range of herbs, especially those that demand excellent drainage, such as lavenders and thymes. In return, herbs' various colors, shapes, and textures make a perfect complement to a wall, softening the hard edges and helping the rocks blend into the landscape.

How High?

A low stone wall (about 2 feet tall or less) is a fun and easy do-it-yourself project. If you need a taller wall, it's a good idea to hire a professional to do the job.

Herbs blend beautifully with all kinds of stone, from rough-textured orange-red sandstone to smooth gray slate to irregularly shaped and colored field stones, so choose whichever material best suits your taste and budget.

The rock wall garden shown here is similar to one we had at the house I grew up in. The wall of that original garden was actually a row of cement blocks — not terribly handsome, but functional, especially since the blocks were set on their sides with the holes facing up and filled with soil. I remember helping my mom plant sedums and other creepers in those pockets. When the plants filled in, you could hardly even see the wall.

For this garden, I've chosen mostly gray- and silver-leaved herbs, including Faassen's catmint, English lavender, yellow lavender cotton, woolly thyme, and woolly yarrow. Along with these, you can use green-leaved thymes, hyssop, and 'Herrenhausen' oregano (with purple-tinged, dark green foliage) for contrast. Through the summer, this planting also offers a variety of pink, purple, blue, and yellow flowers.

Rock Wall Garden

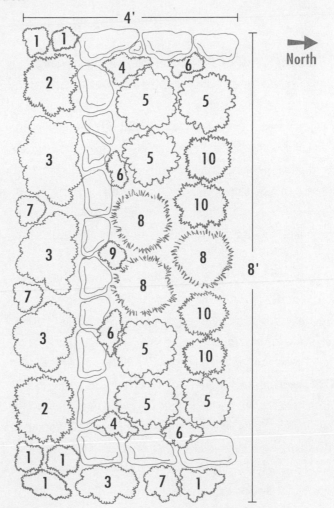

4'

North

8'

Plant List

1. Variegated lemon thyme
   (*Thymus citriodorus* 'Aureus'), 6*
2. Faassen's catmint (*Nepeta* x
   faassenii), 2
3. 'Herrenhausen' oregano
   (*Origanum* 'Herrenhausen'), 3
4. Woolly thyme (*Thymus praecox*
   ssp. *arcticus* 'Lanuginosus'), 2
5. Lavender cotton (*Santolina*
   chamaecyparissus), 6

6. Creeping thyme (*Thymus praecox*
   ssp. *arcticus*), 4
7. Woolly yarrow (*Achillea*
   tomentosa), 3
8. English lavender (*Lavandula*
   angustifolia), 3
9. Caraway thyme (*Thymus*
   herba-barona), 1
10. Hyssop (*Hyssopus officinalis*), 4

*The number after the botanical name
indicates the number of plants needed.

Herbs on an Angle

If installing a wall isn't an option for your site or budget, herbs can still be a good choice for a sloping site. Here are some pointers to help you get your scented slope established:

Select herbs that tolerate dry soil. Choose low-growing, spreading, perennial herbs that will grow rapidly and cover the slope quickly. Bushy or creeping thymes, as well as various perennial oreganos, are perfectly suited to sunny slopes, and they'll provide fragrant foliage and pretty flowers. Yarrows and lavenders also look great on slopes; they are a little taller than thymes and oreganos but make super color accents among the lower-growing herbs.

Prepare the site. Remove any existing sod or weeds, then loosen the soil as best you can (ideally to at least 8 inches) and work in a 2- to 3-inch layer of compost or other organic matter as you dig. Breaking up the soil surface will encourage water to soak in, rather than run off the slope, and the organic matter will hold some of that moisture for your plants' roots.

Start with small plants. If you have a choice between buying a few large herbs or many small herbs to cover your slope, I suggest going for the smaller plants. The cost will probably work out about the same, but the small herbs will be much easier to plant, and I find they settle in more quickly than larger plants.

Use close spacings for quick cover. Before you plant, set your potted herbs on the bank in an arrangement you find pleasing. If possible, space the plants about 6 inches apart, so they'll fill in quickly.

Soak before and after planting. Water your herbs thoroughly before you plant them. I like to submerge the rootball of each herb in a bucket of water until no more bubbles emerge (usually just a minute or two). Water the whole site thoroughly after planting.

Make use of mulch. Apply a layer of mulch to the finished planting to help keep the soil moist. I find shredded bark or licorice root mulch works well in these conditions; lighter weight materials tend to wash off a slope.

CUSTOMIZING THIS DESIGN

This versatile garden, which can turn a problem area into a focal point, is easy to adapt to a variety of sites and climates:

In a shady site. Sun and slopes seem to go together, but you might also need a low wall in a shady spot. If so, replace the suggested plants with low-growing, shade-tolerant herbs: mints, pennyroyal, and sweet woodruff are excellent options.

In cold-winter areas. Most of these herbs are hardy to at least Zone 5, and many can tolerate much more winter cold in the shelter and well-drained soil a rock wall garden can provide. Lavender cotton tends to be a little touchy north of Zone 6, so if you garden in colder areas, consider replacing it with more English lavender or lemon thyme.

For other color choices. Want a more monochromatic look? Select white-flowered hyssop *(Hyssopus officinalis* var. *albus)*, Greek oregano *(Origanum heracleoticum)*, 'The Pearl' yarrow (*Achillea* 'The Pearl'), white creeping thyme (*Thymus praecox* ssp. *arcticus* 'Albus'), and common thyme *(T. vulgaris)*. Look for the catmint cultivar 'Dawn to Dusk', which has pale pink to whitish flowers, trim off the cotton blooms, and you have a (mostly) white garden!

Prefer pink? Choose 'Jean Davis' lavender, 'Dawn to Dusk' catmint, 'Appleblossom' yarrow, and pink-flowered hyssop *(H. officinalis* var. *roseus)* to accent the other rosy-hued herbs.

Hyssop

Catmint

PROBLEM PREVENTION

The sturdy herbs in this design should be trouble-free. None are particularly prone to pests or diseases, especially in the sunny, well-drained conditions of a rock wall garden. Mulching will help to keep weeds to a minimum, especially in the first year or two, until the herbs fill in. Just make sure you keep the mulch away from plant stems; piling it right against the plants can lead to rot.

It's best to start this garden in early spring, if possible, so your herbs have all season to get their roots established before winter comes. I find that fall-planted herbs atop walls tend to be particularly prone to frost heaving (where the alternate freezing and thawing of the soil snaps roots and pushes plant crowns out of the soil). If early spring planting isn't an option, then pay special attention to the Midfall through winter section on page 33 for pointers on helping your herbs survive their first winter.

Early to midspring. After planting your new rock wall garden, water thoroughly, then apply a 1- to 2-inch layer of an organic mulch, such as chopped leaves or shredded bark. Your new rock wall garden won't need much additional care for the first few months. If you get a dry spell, check the soil under the mulch and water when the top inch or two is dry.

Mulch not only keeps down weeds but also conserves moisture and moderates temperatures. Be sure to leave a 2- to 4-inch mulch-free area around the plant to prevent rotting.

Once your herbs are established, spring is a good time to neaten them up. Remove evergreen branches or other winter mulch and clean up any debris that has collected over the months. Cut remaining catmint, oregano, and yarrow top growth to just above the ground. A spring trimming will shape up lavenders, hyssop, bushy thymes, and lavender cotton and promotes dense, bushy growth. Don't be in a hurry, though; wait until mid- or even late spring, when new growth is emerging and the danger of heavy frost is past. That way, you can easily spot and snip out any dead parts and see what is left to trim to shape.

Scatter a ½-inch layer of compost or a few handfuls of a balanced organic fertilizer over the soil every year or two to provide your herbs with a nutrient boost.

Midspring to midsummer. Keep watering new plantings as needed during dry spells. Established herbs can tolerate dry conditions, so there's no need to water them unless rainfall is lacking and the top 2 or 3 inches of soil are dry under the mulch. Pull out any weeds that pop up through the mulch and add more mulch if needed to maintain a 1- to 2-inch layer.

Midsummer to midfall. Enjoy the beauty of your colorful rock wall garden! Water, weed, and add mulch if necessary. If your catmint plants sprawl after their main flush of bloom, leaving an open center, trim them back by half to promote bushier new growth. Cut off the spent yarrow flowers at the base of the plant.

Midfall through winter. As the growing season comes to a close, new plantings benefit from a lightweight winter mulch, such as evergreen branches or a few inches of loose straw. (Discarded Christmas-tree branches are excellent for this purpose.) Wait until the soil is frozen before applying a winter mulch. Established rock wall gardens also benefit from a protective winter mulch, especially north of Zone 6. If you don't mulch, check the garden regularly to see if the alternate freezing and thawing of the soil is pushing any of the plants out of the soil. Pull some loose mulch or soil over to cover any exposed roots and prevent them from drying out; then dig up the displaced plants in spring and replant them at the proper level.

Accenting Your Garden

Don't overlook the value of garden ornaments in adding winter interest to a planting. Statues, gazing balls, unique garden signs, and other accents will be particularly noticeable once your plants go dormant for the winter.

An Herbal Flower Garden

With their colorful flowers and handsome foliage, many herbs make excellent additions to flower beds and borders. In fact, you may be surprised to find out how many plants usually thought of as traditional perennials have also been important in herbal medicine or other herb-related activities. Some examples include catmint, lady's mantle, purple coneflower, and yarrow.

The simple garden shown here does double-duty as an herb garden and a flower garden, since all of the plants can fall into both categories. It's based primarily on soft yellows, pinks, and blues, with a touch of white from the flowers of golden feverfew.

The triangular shape of this garden makes it a good choice for a bright corner, such as the boundary of a property or the area where a deck meets the house. Average, well-drained soil is fine, and ample sun is a must.

Herbal Roses

Not everyone thinks of roses as herbs, but like many of the other flowering herbs, roses have played an important role in herbal history. Over the centuries, both their flowers and fruits (known as hips) have been used in cosmetics, perfumes, and medicines. While there are thousands to choose from, here are three species particularly prized for their herbal uses:

Sweet briar *(Rosa eglanteria)*. Fragrant, yellow-centered, single pink flowers bloom in summer among apple-scented leaves, followed by rounded to oval, orange-red hips. *Zones 4 to 8.*

Apothecary's rose *(R. gallica var. officinalis)*. Large, semi-double, reddish pink summer blooms followed by dark red, rounded hips. *Zones 3 to 8.*

Rugosa rose *(R. rugosa)*. Single purplish pink or white flowers bloom in summer, followed by large, globe-shaped, red hips. *Zones 2 to 8.*

Herbal Flower Garden

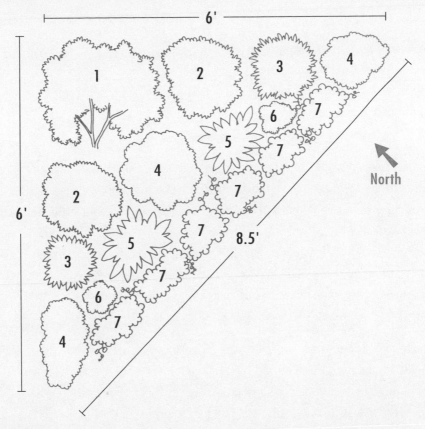

PLANT LIST

1. Apothecary's rose (*Rosa gallica* var. *officinalis*), 1*
2. Faassen's catmint (*Nepeta* x *faassenii*), 2
3. Purple coneflower (*Echinacea purpurea*), 2
4. 'Moonshine' yarrow (*Achillea* 'Moonshine'), 3
5. Mullein (*Verbascum* species), 2
6. Golden feverfew (*Tanacetum parthenium* 'Aureum'), 2
7. 'Moonlight' nasturtium (*Tropaeolum majus* 'Moonlight'), 6

*The number after the botanical name indicates the number of plants needed.

Herbal Arrangements

Many herbs are ideal for creating beautiful and fragrant bouquets. While you are gathering flowers, don't forget to harvest some foliage, too; leaves with interesting colors, scents, or textures add an extra element of interest to a bouquet.

Gathering the Herbs

Gather herbs early in the morning, if possible, before the heat of the day starts to dry them out. Make clean cuts with a sharp pair of scissors or pruning shears, snipping just above a leaf or leaf pair. Place each cut stem into a container of tepid water right away.

Once you bring the flowers and foliage indoors, recut the base of all the stems at an angle while they are still underwater. Remove any leaves that will be under the water line of your finished arrangement.

Making the Arrangement

Herbs look lovely simply placed loose in a vase, crock, or other narrow-mouthed container. For a more formal arrangement, soak a piece of floral foam in water and set it in a waterproof bowl or tray. (Foam works best for herbs with stiff stems; soft-stemmed herbs such as nasturtiums will break or bend if you try to push them into the foam.) Add a commercial floral preservative to the water of finished arrangements or use a few drops of bleach and a pinch of sugar. Check the water level daily.

Enjoying a Bonus

You may find that some herbs actually form roots in the water or floral foam. (If an herb roots in the foam, don't try to pull it out; just cut off the piece of foam with the roots in it.) Plant the rooted stems, foam and all, in moist potting soil and you'll have new herbs to grow or share!

CUSTOMIZING THIS DESIGN

Most of the perennials in this design are cold-hardy through Zone 4, so this low-maintenance herbal flower garden would grow well in a variety of climates. If you are interested in customizing it for your particular tastes, here are some ideas:

Change the color scheme. Flower gardens are a fun place to experiment with different color schemes. For instance, most of the herbs in this garden come in white-flowered or white-variegated forms, so you could easily turn this into an elegant white garden (just choose a different rose). An all-pink garden is another possibility. In this case, though, you might want to replace the nasturtiums with pink petunias or another pink annual; most "pink" nasturtiums are actually an orangey pink that clashes with the bright reddish pink of the rose.

Nasturtiums

Multiple mullein choices. You're not likely to find a wide variety of mulleins at your local garden center, but, happily, these plants are easy to grow from seed. If you like yellow flowers, try *V. bombyciferum*, a biennial with silvery leaves, or *V. chaixii*, a perennial with green leaves. Another selection of the latter species — *V. chaixii* var. *album* — has white flowers with the same fuzzy purple centers. A favorite of mine is a seed strain known as 'Southern Charm'. It produces quite a few yellows but also some plants with lovely rosy pink or buff-orange blooms.

PROBLEM PREVENTION

Pests and diseases rarely bother the plants included in this herbal flower garden, as long as the herbs are growing in well-drained soil. Apothecary's rose sometimes shows signs of powdery mildew in the form of dusty white or gray patches on the leaves. To control this fungal disease, spray the foliage with fungicidal soap or horticultural oil (1 tablespoon of oil per gallon of water); reapply every few weeks if you see more patches develop on the leaves.

This colorful collection of flowering herbs thrives in a sunny, well-drained site. You can start the garden just about any time the ground isn't frozen, but ideal planting seasons are from early to midspring and late summer to midfall. Summer planting is all right, too, but you'll need to pay extra careful attention to regular watering during dry spells.

Early to midspring. This is a good time to set out the rosebush and perennial herbs according to the plan. Water thoroughly after planting; then apply a 2-inch layer of chopped leaves or other organic mulch. Leave a 2- to 4-inch-diameter unmulched circle around the base of each plant.

Once your herbal flower garden is established, spring is cleanup time. Cut down any remaining top growth on the perennial herbs, and pull out weeds and the remains of the nasturtiums if you didn't do that the previous fall.

The rose will also benefit from some yearly attention in late winter or early spring. First, prune out any dead growth, then trim back leggy shoots to shape the plant.

Once you're finished with cleanup and pruning, rake off the loose mulch. Spread a ½-inch layer of compost over the whole garden (try not to pile it on the crowns of the perennials), or scatter all-purpose organic fertilizer over the soil, following the application rate suggested on the package. Replace the material you raked off and add fresh mulch if needed to keep the layer 2 inches thick.

Midspring to midsummer. Around your last frost date, sow the nasturtium seeds or set out transplants. Pull out any weeds that have managed to make their way through the mulch layer. If rain is lacking, check the soil under the mulch. When the top 3 inches of soil are dry, it's time to water.

Midsummer to midfall. Regular deadheading will help keep your herbal flower garden looking good for months. After their first flush of bloom, cut your catmint plants back by half to promote bushier growth and some rebloom. Cut yarrow stems to the ground when their blooms fade, and clip off spent purple coneflower blooms just above the uppermost set of leaves. Mullein will self-sow, too, but it's good to have a few seedlings, since biennial mulleins usually die after flowering. The lowest blooms on the spike are usually setting seed by the time the top flowers are finishing, so let a few seed capsules turn brown and drop seed, then cut off the whole spike at the ground.

Don't deadhead the rose, of course, or you'll miss out on those beautiful fruits! Just prune lightly after bloom to thin out crowded stems and to improve the plant's shape.

Midfall through winter. As the season winds down, keep deadheading regularly. Nasturtiums can usually take a light frost, but once a freeze leaves the plants limp, you can pull them out or cut the stems off right at ground level. During the first winter, you might want to protect your new planting with a generous layer of loose straw or evergreen boughs, especially if you live where snow cover is not reliable.

On golden feverfew, pinch off individual blooms or shear the whole plant back to about 3 inches above the ground after it blooms. After two or three weeks, you'll have a new mound of bright yellow foliage to enjoy.

Adding Year-Round Interest

Seed heads and colorful fruits add a lot to a garden's winter interest, but you can also employ other tricks to keep a planting going through the off-season. Shrubs, perennials, and ground covers with evergreen foliage are a great choice. Low-growing dwarf conifers, for instance, come in a wide range of heights, habits, and foliage colors, including greens, blue-greens, and yellow-gold. These versatile plants blend well with many herbs, since they share a need for ample sun and well-drained soil.

A SCENTED SHADE GARDEN

Trying to grow grass under trees can be a real hassle, but what other options do you have? Why not turn that problem area into a beautiful shade garden? Shade-tolerant annuals and perennials add height, texture, and seasonal interest to your landscape while eliminating mowing chores in that area. And when you include shade-adapted herbs, you enjoy the additional bonus of fragrance as well as pretty flowers and attractive foliage.

In this garden, I've highlighted some of my favorite shade-loving herbs, as well as more traditional shade-garden choices. I know some gardeners cringe at the idea of planting sweet woodruff because of its spreading nature. But in my garden, I find it invaluable as a ground cover around the base of mature trees, where the summer shade is too dense and the soil is too dry for more delicate plants. Yes, it does spread rapidly when it gets out where there is more light and moisture, but it's not hard to cut it back or pull it out in spring to make room for annuals. And while sweet woodruff is vigorous enough to choke out delicate woodland wildflowers, I find that hostas and mints are usually tough enough to hold their own against it.

Sweet woodruff

White — in either flowers or foliage — is a wonderful addition to shade gardens, since it really brightens up a dark area. Green-and-white combinations also have a fresh, cool look that is a welcome sight on sultry summer days. And when you include plants with green-and-white-variegated foliage, such as pineapple mint, you get to enjoy the effect all season long.

Keep in mind that this garden is suited for the shade under a deciduous tree, not an evergreen one. Evergreens cast deep, year-round shade that few plants can tolerate. A much wider range of plants can tolerate deciduous shade, especially since they get ample light and moisture in spring, until the trees' leaves are fully expanded.

Scented Shade Garden

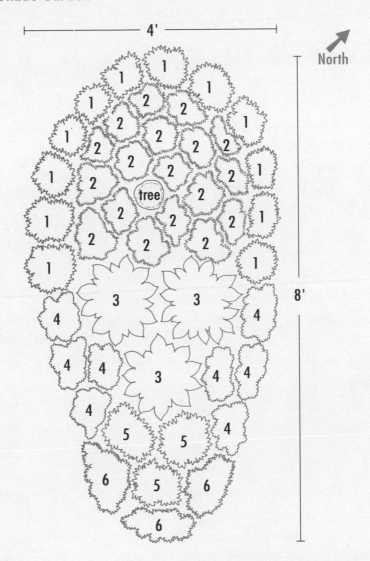

Plant List

1. White impatiens *(Impatiens wallerana)*, 12*
2. Sweet woodruff *(Galium odoratum)*, 18
3. Hostas (*Hosta* species), 3
4. Pennyroyal *(Mentha pulegium)*, 8
5. Pineapple mint *(Mentha suaveolens 'Variegata')*, 3
6. Peppermint geranium *(Pelargonium tomentosum)*, 3

*The number after the botanical name indicates the number of plants needed.

Shady Strategies: Planting Pockets

General gardening wisdom recommends that when you're starting a new garden, you should loosen the soil in the whole planting area and work organic matter evenly into the root zone. When you're planting a garden under a tree, however, that isn't necessarily the best approach. You still need to loosen the soil, but you don't want to damage the tree's feeder roots, which tend to spread near the soil surface. I've had good luck with the technique of creating planting pockets — individual planting holes enriched with compost or other organic matter.

To create planting pockets, use a trowel or small spade to dig individual holes two to three times wider than the rootball of each herb and about as deep. Work a handful of compost into the soil at the bottom of the hole. In addition, mix a handful of two or compost into the soil you remove from each hole before filling it back in. After planting, water thoroughly and then add a mulch of chopped leaves or other organic material to keep the soil moist. This enriched, moist soil will encourage your shade-loving herbs to fill in rapidly.

CUSTOMIZING THIS DESIGN

The plants in this garden are tough and cold-hardy at least through Zone 5, so they should perform well in a variety of climates.

Add bulbs for early color. Spring bulbs are a perfect addition to this garden, since they will thrive in the ample early season sunlight and go dormant by the time deciduous trees shade the site. Good choices include small bulbs such as crocuses, daffodils, grape hyacinths (*Muscari* species), and snowdrops (*Galanthus* species). As the perennials and herbs emerge, they will mask the yellowing foliage of the maturing bulbs.

Hosta options. With thousands of different hostas to choose from, what you decide to plant is really a matter of personal taste. Cultivars with white-centered or white-edged leaves would look particularly good in this garden. August lily *(Hosta plantaginea)* is another possibility: Its leaves are plain green, but it produces pure white, fragrant, trumpet-shaped blooms in late summer.

PROBLEM PREVENTION

Few pests or disease will bother these tough plants, so most of the problem prevention involves the plants themselves! Sweet woodruff, pennyroyal, and pineapple mint are all willing spreaders, so be prepared to control them if needed. Mostly, that means cutting them back or pulling some out to keep them from crowding out the annuals and perennials.

Also, this garden will be surrounded by grass. To make maintenance easier, I recommend installing some kind of edging — perhaps a row of bricks or a plastic or metal edging strip — around the perimeter of the bed. Otherwise, you'll have to trim around the garden several times during the season to keep the grass from creeping in and the herbs from creeping out into your lawn!

Pennyroyal

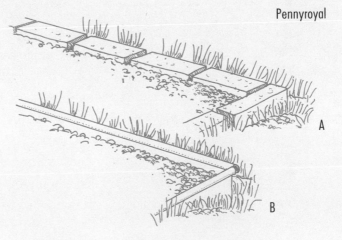

Edge herb beds with bricks (A) or a plastic or metal edging strip (B) to keep your herbs confined to their bed and your grass in the lawn where it belongs.

CARE THROUGH THE SEASONS

This garden is a great way to add color and fragrance to an otherwise hard-to-maintain area under a deciduous tree. While most of these plants prefer a steady supply of soil moisture, they can tolerate somewhat dry conditions once established, especially if they get a generous layer of mulch. Keep in mind that few herbs thrive in the deep, all-season shade cast by evergreens.

Fall planting is perfect for the perennials in this garden. The warm soil but cooler air temperatures and ample moisture are ideal for encouraging root growth. Plus, the plants will be in place to take advantage of spring sun before the tree leafs out for the season. The seasonal care guidelines below follow the fall-planting approach, but if you'd prefer to start in spring, just check the Midfall through winter section on page 45 for planting tips.

Early to midspring. As the weather warms up, take a few minutes to clean up any debris that has accumulated and cut back remaining top growth on the perennials. If you didn't pull out the annuals (impatiens and peppermint geraniums) in the fall, do so now. Once the garden is cleaned up, rake off the loose mulch.

If you live where summers tend to be dry, this is a good time to plan ahead for summer watering by laying a soaker hose. Start with a ring around the perimeter, about 1 foot in from the edge, and then snake it back and forth among the hostas and pineapple mint if you have any extra hose left.

Pull any weeds that are visible and spread a ½- to 1-inch layer of compost over the whole site (including the soaker hose). Add more mulch if needed to maintain a 2-inch-deep layer. (Try to avoid piling mulch on the crowns of the emerging perennials.) The yearly top-dressing of compost provides a small but steady supply of nutrients, which is ideal for these plants, so fertilize regularly only if your soil is in poor condition.

Midspring to midsummer. After all danger of frost is past, set out the impatiens and the peppermint geraniums. Water them thoroughly and then add more mulch around them, keeping the mulch an inch or two away from their stems. Pull any weeds you see before they set seed. If the weather is dry, check under the mulch; water when the top 2 or 3 inches of soil are dry.

Midsummer to midfall. If rainfall is lacking, water as needed. If any weeds have the nerve to pop up through the mulch, grab them while they are still small.

Sometimes sweet woodruff will blacken or die back during warm, humid weather. If you see this happening to your plants, remove all the top growth to about an inch above the ground (a string trimmer is handy for this job). Within a few weeks, you'll have a carpet of fresh new growth.

Midfall through winter. The fall season (specifically, early to midfall) is a good time to get this garden started. Once you've removed the existing vegetation, set out the perennial plants according to the plan. (See Shady Strategies on page 42 for tips on planting under trees.) Water thoroughly; then add a 1-inch topdressing of compost and another 1 or 2 inches of an organic mulch, such as chopped leaves. North of Zone 6 you might want to protect the new planting with a loose winter mulch, such as straw or evergreen boughs, once the ground freezes.

If your garden is already established, there isn't much to do in this season, except to take cuttings from or dig up the peppermint geranium plants if you want to keep them through the winter. If it looks like your first fall frost will be a heavy one, I suggest pulling out the impatiens before they get hit. Once the plants have frozen and thawed, they are very slimy and hard to grip! If your plants do get frosted, either cut them off at ground level or just leave them in place to break down over winter.

Recycled Clippings Are Crafters' Treasures

If you enjoy making crafts, save the green tops of sweet woodruff when you cut them and set them in a warm, dark, airy place to dry. Once they are fully dry, you'll notice their sweet, vanilla-like scent. Crumble the leaves into potpourri or use them in sachets or herbal pillows.

AN HERBAL KITCHEN GARDEN

No, it's not a garden *in* your kitchen — but it's almost as good! A kitchen garden is a place to grow a mix of herbs, vegetables, and even fruit: anything that you might use frequently in your cooking. I must admit that I'm not much of a vegetable gardener — or a cook, for that matter — but I do enjoy having a little garden like this one to harvest from. It's fun to walk outside and snip a few herbs and greens to spruce up a store-bought salad or even a frozen dinner.

I think the key to getting the most from a garden such as this is careful placement. It must be convenient to the house, so you can quickly pop out and snip what you need. Keep your main-harvest crops — beans, corn, peppers, and other veggies you use in quantity — out in the main vegetable garden; the kitchen garden is the place to go when you need "a little of this and a little of that." Traditional vegetable gardens are usually sited in a not-very-visible spot, because they generally aren't very exciting to look at. But since a kitchen garden belongs near the house, it's important to have it be handsome as well as productive.

The garden shown on the opposite page is a simple but flexible design of three square beds that are 3 feet on each side. With a bed this size, it's easy to reach into the center from all sides, which makes maintenance and harvesting much simpler. The beds can be right at ground level, but for extra interest make them into raised beds framed with stones, timbers, or even brick. Set all three in a row or place them at a 90 degree angle to fit in a corner of the yard. Leave a space at least 2 feet wide between each for paths.

Looking to create a little more interest? Consider turning each kitchen garden bed 45 degrees to create a pattern of three diamonds. Or make a series of circular beds with similar dimensions. Either way, you can use the same planting plans suggested opposite.

Herbal Kitchen Garden

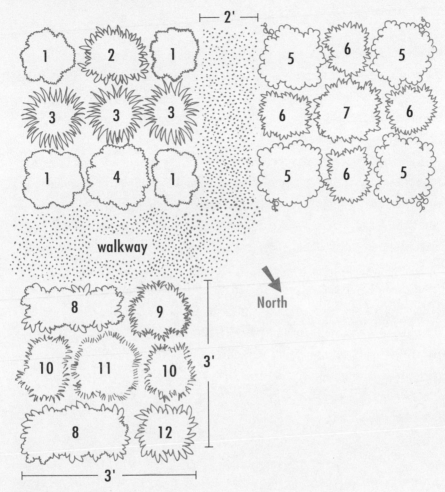

walkway

North

PLANT LIST

1. English thyme *(Thymus vulgaris)*, 4*
2. Culinary sage *(Salvia officinalis)*, 1
3. Chives *(Allium schoenoprasum)*, 3
4. Greek oregano *(Origanum heracleoticum)*, 1
5. Nasturtium *(Tropaeolum majus)*, 4
6. Basil *(Ocimum basilicum)*, 4
7. Tomato (any type), 1
8. Mesclun, 2 packets
9. French Tarragon *(Artemisia dracunculus)*, 1
10. Dill *(Anethum graveolens)*, 1 packet
11. Rosemary *(Rosmarinus officinalis)*, 1
12. French sorrel *(Rumex scutatus)*, 1

*The number after the botanical name indicates the number of plants needed.

Mix It Up with Mesclun

If you're looking for a way to liven up your salads, mesclun is a great place to start. Mesclun is simply a bunch of different greens blended together as seed and sown in patches or wide rows for easy harvesting. Just a handful or two of mesclun mix can really liven up a bowl of plain old lettuce!

You can purchase mesclun mixes from most seed companies, and that's a good way to try out various combinations without buying lots of different seeds. You can also make your own mesclun mix, but there is no exact recipe for doing so. Many mixes start with a base of a few types of looseleaf lettuce (usually one red and one green); after that, it's a matter of taste. A traditional mix, for instance, generally includes arugula, chervil, and endive for a blend of mild flavors with a bit of zip. If you enjoy somewhat stronger flavors, try adding red and green chicory, dandelion, and mustard.

To make your own mesclun mix, start with two packets of lettuce seed and add four half-packets of other greens of your choice. Blend the seed thoroughly; then sow it directly in the garden.

Use scissors to gather the tender mesclun leaves when they are 3 to 4 inches tall, cutting about ½ inch above the ground. Harvest the young leaves frequently to encourage new growth.

CUSTOMIZING THIS DESIGN

This simple design is so flexible that the possibilities for customizing it are almost endless. Here are just a few ideas:

In a damp-soil site. If you have a sunny site but soggy or heavy clay soil, simply frame in each square with 4- to 5-inch-high stone, wood, or brick walls and fill them with a mixture of good garden soil (available from garden centers) and compost. The raised beds will provide the loose, well-drained conditions these plants thrive in.

Be adventurous with basil. Sure, we all think of the traditional sweet basil that's so great with tomatoes, but that's just the beginning. 'Mammoth', for instance, has especially large leaves that are ideal for rolling around fillings, such as cream cheese. Purple-leaved basils are particularly pretty: I like the crinkled leaves of 'Purple Ruffles' and the smooth foliage of 'Red Rubin'. 'Spicy Globe' is a green dwarf form that produces dense, compact mounds of tiny leaves. There are many other interesting basil flavors to try, such as 'Anise', 'Cinnamon', and 'Lemon'. With room for four basil plants in this garden, why not plant a variety?

A salad bar in your backyard. If you enjoy summer salads, consider customizing your plant choices to that end. You could, for instance, replace the thyme, sage, and oregano plants with looseleaf lettuces and choose a cherry-type tomato ('Sweet 100' is a long-standing favorite in my family) for bite-sized fruits. Grow purple-leaved basils, such as 'Purple Ruffles' basil, and use their foliage to add color and flavor to vinegars for dressing the salads. Other easy-to-grow salad plants include corn salad *(Valerianella locusta)*, fennel, radishes, and salad burnet *(Poterium sanguisorba)*.

'Purple Ruffles'
basil

PROBLEM PREVENTION

Give this kitchen garden a spot with full sun and average, well-drained soil, and it will reward you with a wealth of ingredients for your summertime meals. None of these plants is particularly susceptible to serious problems. Just wait until the weather has warmed up before you set out your basil plants. They sulk in cool air and seem to take awhile to recover once they've been chilled. Also, be sure to remove the spent flowers of the chives, dill, and sorrel, or you'll find them popping up everywhere in your garden next year.

If you do see any pests, remove them by hand or knock them off the plants with a blast of water. You're growing these herbs and vegetables to eat, so you sure don't want to use chemicals on them!

CARE THROUGH THE SEASONS

You can set up this garden any time of year, but the best time to plant the perennial herbs is from early to midspring or late summer to early fall. Fill in with the annuals and frost-tender plants in later spring.

Early to midspring. If you decide to start this garden in spring, you can set out the hardy perennial herbs — chives, Greek oregano, sage, French sorrel, tarragon, and thyme — whenever plants are available in nurseries or by mail order. In following years, use this time to clean up any debris that has gathered in the garden. Remove the remaining top growth on the chives, sorrel, and tarragon and trim the oregano stems to just above the ground. Once new growth emerges, trim sage plants to shape them (after removing any dead growth). Shear thyme plants back by about half to promote bushy new growth.

Dill can take some cold, and it grows best when sown directly in the garden, so early to midspring is a good time to plant it. Scatter the seed evenly over one of its two allotted 1-foot-square spaces; press it lightly into the soil surface or cover it with a sprinkling of soil. Keep the area evenly moist until seedlings appear.

Dill

Roughly two weeks before your last frost date, make the first sowing of the mesclun mix in one of its two allotted spaces. Give it the same treatment as your dill.

Since you'll be harvesting these herbs, they'll need a generous supply of readily available nutrients to produce ample top growth. Give each bed some all-purpose organic fertilizer each spring.

Midspring to midsummer. About three weeks after your first sowing of dill and mesclun, sow more seed in the remaining space allotted for each. This staggered planting will extend your harvest for both crops well into summer.

Wait until around your average last frost date to sow the nasturtium seeds directly in the garden or to set out transplants. A week or two later, when all danger of frost has passed, set out your tomato, basil, and rosemary plants. (If you'd rather sow your basil outdoors, sow in mid- to late spring, cover with a sprinkling of soil, and keep evenly moist; the seed will germinate as soon as warm conditions arrive.) Both the tomatoes and basil appreciate a bit of extra fertility, so work a handful or two of compost into the bottom of their planting holes. (Don't add it to the adjacent nasturtiums, though, or they might produce lush leaves but no flowers!)

Once you've set out or sown all of the plants, remove any weeds; then add a 2-inch layer of an organic mulch, such as chopped leaves, over the soil. Leave a 2- to 4-inch-wide mulch-free ring around the base of each plant. If rainfall is lacking, be sure to water. It's especially important to keep newly seeded spots moist.

Start harvesting your mesclun greens when they are 3 to 4 inches tall. Pinch off sprigs of the other herbs as you need them.

Midsummer to midfall. Continue harvesting your herbs and vegetables whenever you need them. Don't forget to enjoy the nasturtium leaves and flowers in your salads, too; they'll add a peppery taste.

When the dill and mesclun leaves turn bitter or tough, pull out the plants and toss them into your compost pile. Cover the bare space with mulch. For a fall harvest, about 10 weeks before your first frost date, pull back the mulch and make another sowing of dill and mesclun in some of the empty spaces; repeat three weeks later.

During dry spells, check the soil under the mulch; water if the top 2 or 3 inches are dry.

Midfall through winter. Keep up with the harvesting — most of these herbs still taste great even after light frosts. If you plan to keep your rosemary plant, though, you'll generally need to bring it indoors before the first frost if you live north of Zone 8. (Some cultivars, such as 'Arp', can reportedly overwinter outdoors in most areas of Zone 7.)

Most of the perennial herbs in this garden are cold-hardy at least through Zone 5, so they won't need much in the way of winter protection except in colder zones. If snow cover isn't dependable in your area, consider protecting them with a mulch of loose straw or evergreen branches once the ground freezes.

A MOONLIGHT HERB GARDEN

After a long day at the office, it's a pleasure to steal a few minutes to stroll around your garden. Unfortunately, you don't get to see much of the color once the sun sets; that has to wait for sunny weekend days. Well, you *can* have a garden to enjoy all week long: The secret is to include plants that have white or light-colored blooms or silvery leaves. These special plants are ideal for evening viewing, since they'll reflect any available light.

In this garden, I've included a selection of easy-to-grow herbs, as well as white-flowered Madagascar periwinkle, an easy-to-grow annual that thrives in the same sunny, average-to-dry soil conditions the herbs prefer. The Madagascar periwinkle's flat-faced flowers are a clean, pure white that looks great against the dark green foliage during the day, and at night they almost glow. This garden also includes the cheerful white blooms of feverfew and garlic chives, as well as the pale yellow flowers and silvery gray foliage of 'Moonlight' yarrow. Shrubby clumps of 'Powis Castle' artemisia and 'Hidcote' lavender continue the silvery foliage theme, along with the showy, white,

Garlic chives

woolly rosettes of mullein. Silver thyme contributes aromatic, white-edged, gray-green leaves, as well as pink summertime flowers to the collection.

The garden shown here would look lovely planted at the edge of a patio or around a deck — wherever you can sit and unwind on a summer evening. In fact, you could easily flip the plan over to create two symmetrical beds for flanking three sides of your sitting area. These plants are just tall enough to provide a bit of an enclosure while not obstructing your view beyond.

Wildlife by Moonlight

Besides adding beauty in their own right, many of these flowers offer another benefit: They often attract gorgeous night-flying moths, so you'll get to enjoy the visiting wildlife as well as the plants!

Moonlight Herb Garden

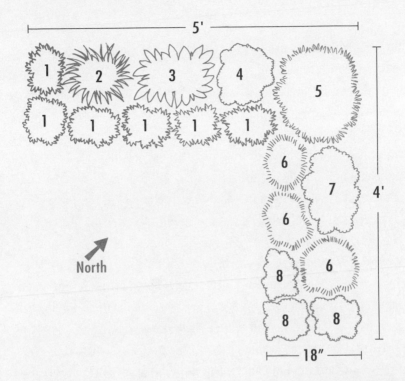

PLANT LIST

1. White Madagascar periwinkle (*Catharanthus roseus*), 6*
2. Garlic chives *(Allium tuberosum)*, 1
3. Mullein *(Verbascum bombyciferum)*, 1
4. Feverfew *(Tanacetum parthenium)*, 1
5. 'Powis Castle' artemisia (*Artemisia* 'Powis Castle'), 1

6. 'Hidcote' lavender (*Lavandula angustifolia* 'Hidcote'), 3
7. 'Moonlight' yarrow (*Achillea millefolium* 'Moonlight'), 1
8. Silver thyme (*Thymus* x *citriodorus* 'Argenteus'), 3

*The number after the botanical name indicates the number of plants needed.

Even More Evening Flowers

Looking for other flowers to enjoy in your moonlight garden? Here are three of my favorites:

Magic primrose *(Oenothera glazioviana)*. During its first year, this biennial, or short-lived perennial, produces a rather nondescript rosette of narrow, medium-green leaves. The following season, though, it sends up a long leafy stalk loaded with buds from midsummer well into fall. Each evening, about half an hour before dark, I make it a point to go out and watch that night's buds quiver for a minute or two and then whirl open in just a few seconds. As an added bonus, the beautiful yellow blooms also release a pleasant scent.

Night phlox *(Zaluzianskya capensis)*. This charming little annual isn't much to look at during the day: just a clump of small, narrow, bright green leaves and hard-to-see maroon buds. But at night, the petals fold back to show their pure white insides and release their sweet scent.

White heliotrope *(Heliotropium arborescens)*. You'll usually find heliotrope in shades of purple, but I particularly favor the white-flowered kind; with its baby-powder scent, it seems more fragrant than the purple ones, especially in the evening. Plus, the white flowers of this tender perennial stand out against the bright green leaves, even in the least amount of light.

CUSTOMIZING THIS DESIGN

This simple design is well suited for skirting the border of a sunny deck or patio. All of the perennials in this design are generally hardy in Zone 5 and south, except perhaps for the 'Powis Castle' artemisia (Zones 6 to 9). If this plant doesn't do well in your area, consider replacing it with something else that's silvery but a little hardier — such as 'Valerie Finnis' artemisia (Zones 5 to 9). Here are some more ideas for personalizing this design:

Options for lavender lovers. To get even more evening enjoyment from this garden, you could search out a white-flowered form of English lavender *(Lavandula angustifolia)* to replace the suggested purple-flowered cultivar 'Hidcote'. 'Alba' is similar but somewhat taller (to 3 feet); 'Nana Alba' also has white blooms but is much more compact (to about 8 inches).

Lavender

If you don't have luck overwintering lavender in your garden, treat it like an annual and set out new plants each year. In that case, consider trying some of the more tender species, since you'll be replacing them anyway. Some possibilities include lacy-leaved branched lavender *(L. multifida)* or the silvery white leaves of woolly lavender *(L. lanata);* both of these usually overwinter only in frost-free areas.

Annual ideas. If you're looking for an alternate edging for your moonlight garden, lots of annual options cry out for use. Consider the lacy silver foliage of dusty miller *(Senecio cineraria)*, the fuzzy white blooms of 'Summer Snow' ageratum *(Ageratum houstonianum* 'Summer Snow'), or a white-flowered petunia, such as 'Celebrity White'. Sweet alyssum *(Lobularia maritima)* is especially nice as a low edging, since its small, clustered blooms release a delightfully sweet scent.

PROBLEM PREVENTION

Select a site with full sun and well-drained soil, and your moonlight herb garden will thrive. None of these plants is particularly prone to pest or disease problems, except perhaps for rot in very rainy or humid conditions. In fact, the only real problem you may face is that some of the herbs produce unwanted offspring through self-sowing. Several of these plants, including feverfew, garlic chives, and mullein, produce lots of seed and can quickly become weedy if you don't take steps to control them. Fortunately, it's not difficult: Just remove the spent flowers before the seeds have a chance to ripen. For more tips, see Care through the Seasons on the following page.

CARE THROUGH THE SEASONS

You can set out the perennial herbs in this garden just about any time the ground isn't frozen, but they'll settle in best if you plant them in early to midspring or late summer to early fall. If you don't get around to making the garden until summer and the plants are all available, you can certainly go ahead and plant then, but you'll need to pay special attention to watering.

Early to midspring. This is a great time to set out a new garden, so gather your perennial herbs and get them in the ground. (But hold off on setting out the Madagascar periwinkle plants until the weather warms up.) After planting, water the soil thoroughly. Add a 2-inch layer of chopped leaves or other organic mulch, leaving a 2- to 4-inch-wide circle without mulch around the base of each plant.

Spring is also the season for a bit of cleanup in established gardens. If there's any top growth left on the yarrow, feverfew, or garlic chives, cut it to the ground to make room for new shoots. Also yank out the old Madagascar periwinkle plants, if you haven't already done so. Remove any tattered leaves from the mullein rosette.

Artemisia

Tidy up your artemisia, lavender, and thyme plants with a bit of pruning. In most areas, it's best to wait until midspring (or even late spring) for this, when the danger of heavy frost is past. Cut out any dead stems; then trim each plant to shape it, making your cuts just above emerging new growth.

Most of the herbs in this garden don't need lots of nutrients, so they can get by on a ½-inch layer of compost or a scattering of all-purpose organic fertilizer every other spring. You may notice that your mulch layer has thinned out since the previous fall; add more mulch if needed to maintain a 2-inch cover.

Midspring to midsummer. Wait a week or two after your last frost date to set out the Madagascar periwinkle plants. They like warm weather and will sulk if you set them out when the soil is still cold. (If you don't know the last frost date in your area, ask other gardeners in your neighborhood or check with your local garden center or Cooperative Extension Service.) Other than that, there's not much to do. Just add more mulch as needed and pull out any weeds that pop through. The herbs in this garden don't need a lot of moisture, so you won't need to water unless rainfall has been lacking. Pull away some mulch and use a trowel to check the soil. If the top 3 inches are dry, it's time to water. (Actually, garlic chives seem to prefer a bit more moisture, so it wouldn't hurt to hand-water them more often during dry spells.) Keep in mind that silver-leaved plants are naturally adapted to hot, dry spots, so they're not used to having water standing on their leaves as it can if you use overhead irrigation. Soaker hoses are the best option: For more information, see Watering on page 136.

Midsummer to midfall. To keep your herbs looking their best, remove spent flowers regularly. This is especially important with feverfew, which can self-sow with abandon. You can pinch off individual blooms, but that gets a bit tedious; I find it's easier to shear the whole plant back to about 3 inches above the ground after the main flush of bloom. After two or three weeks, you'll have a neat mound of fresh green foliage to enjoy — and maybe even more flowers. Mullein self-sows, too, but it's good to have a few seedlings, since the parent plant generally dies after flowering. The lowest blooms on the spike are usually setting seed by the time the top flowers are finishing, so let a few seed capsules turn brown and drop seed, and then cut off the whole spike at the ground.

Midfall through winter. Keep deadheading your herbs as needed through the fall, especially the garlic chives, which should be finishing their bloom season. Once frost blackens your Madagascar periwinkle plants, you can pull them out and add them to your compost pile. After the ground freezes, consider protecting new plantings with a lightweight winter mulch, such as evergreen branches or a few inches of loose straw. North of Zone 6, established gardens can benefit from this as well.

AN HERBAL COTTAGE GARDEN

The term *cottage gardens* evokes different responses from different gardeners. Some think of them as haphazard collections of odds-and-ends, while others appreciate their cheerful mayhem. It is possible, however, to create a cottage garden that is a happy medium between the formality of a carefully planned border and the weedy, forgotten look of a garden left to its own devices.

There are three keys to creating a garden that looks cared for but still casual. First, include multiples of a few plants to give some repetition to the design. You don't have to plant everything in groups of three or five or seven, but if you do include a few groupings, you'll avoid the uneven look that a one-of-this-and-one-of-that garden often has.

Another secret to successful cottage gardening is allowing the plants to seed around a bit once they are established. The seedlings will pop up in the most surprising places, often creating beautiful combinations you never would have thought of. The randomness of self-sowing also helps to blend the different plant groupings, so they don't look isolated and formal. If you like, you can help the process along by clipping off ripe seed heads and shaking them over bare spots in your garden.

The third thing I've discovered about cottage gardening is the importance of "editing" in keeping the balance between casual and chaos. Now that I've suggested that you allow your herbs to self-sow, I also have to warn you not to allow *all* of them to set seed *all* of the time. Let only a few flowers per plant set seed, decide which seedlings you want to keep, and ruthlessly remove unwanted seedlings while they are still small. Keeping a neat, clipped edge around the garden also works wonders for improving its appearance.

This L-shaped garden would look great in the corner of a yard, or perhaps bordering a deck, porch, or patio. I'm a firm believer in the value of benches in the garden, so I've included one in this design to encourage you to get up-close-and-personal with your beautiful, fragrant herbs.

Herbal Cottage Garden

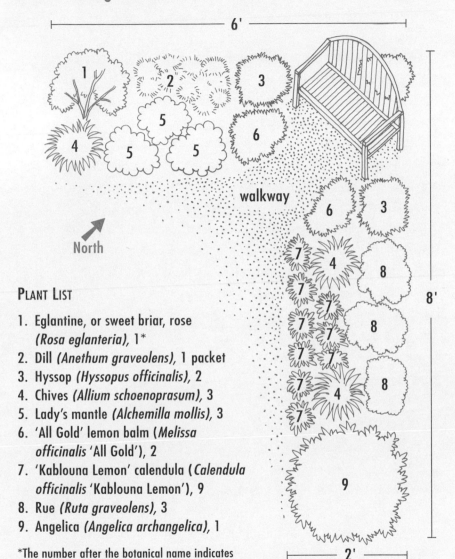

North

walkway

6'

8'

2'

PLANT LIST

1. Eglantine, or sweet briar, rose (*Rosa eglanteria*), 1*
2. Dill (*Anethum graveolens*), 1 packet
3. Hyssop (*Hyssopus officinalis*), 2
4. Chives (*Allium schoenoprasum*), 3
5. Lady's mantle (*Alchemilla mollis*), 3
6. 'All Gold' lemon balm (*Melissa officinalis* 'All Gold'), 2
7. 'Kablouna Lemon' calendula (*Calendula officinalis* 'Kablouna Lemon'), 9
8. Rue (*Ruta graveolens*), 3
9. Angelica (*Angelica archangelica*), 1

*The number after the botanical name indicates the number of plants needed.

Seed Exchanges

Besides deadheading, there *is* another way to keep your garden from filling up with seedlings: Collect the seed and share it with other gardeners! Seed exchanges are a super way to find a home for your extras in return for seeds of new plants you'd like to try.

Many plant societies offer a seed exchange for their members. Two that are particularly good for herb aficionados are the Flower and Herb Exchange and the Herb Society of America. (You'll find their contact information in Herbal Resources on page 149.)

Every exchange has its own guidelines for donating and requesting seed. Some allow you to request seed (usually for a small fee), even if you haven't contributed any. But donors often get their orders filled first or receive extra packets, so it's definitely worth your time to collect ripe seed, place it in labeled paper envelopes, and send it in according to the guidelines. Then, wait for the seed list to arrive and be prepared to have fun choosing from all the exciting selections!

CUSTOMIZING THIS DESIGN

Part of the fun of cottage gardening is adding personal touches, such as your favorite bench or special plants shared by friends. Here are some other ideas for personalizing this design:

Southern suggestions. A number of the plants in this design — especially the angelica and calendulas — won't thrive in the heat of a sunny southern summer. In areas south of Zone 7, consider replacing the angelica with an additional rose, such as rugosa rose *(Rosa rugosa),* or perhaps another large perennial, such as hollyhock *(Alcea rugosa).* And instead of the calendulas, choose another low-growing annual that performs well in your climate. Verbenas *(Verbena* species) are excellent choices.

Consider the rose. I've recommended sweet briar rose for this garden because of its old-fashioned single pink flowers, dark green, fruity-scented leaves, and scarlet fruits. It also tends to resist pests and disease — a big plus! But there are many other wonderful roses to choose from. For more information on some of the best, see Herbal Roses on page 34. Of course, there are thousands more species and cultivars to choose from. Talk to other gardeners in your neighborhood to find out which roses perform well in your area.

PROBLEM PREVENTION

Most of the plants I've included in this design will readily produce many offspring by self-sowing. While you want to allow *some* seeding, this garden can become a jumble after just a year or two if you don't take steps to minimize seed production. On the angelica, chives, and dill, clip off the spent flower clusters as soon as you see them. Once new blooms stop forming, allow just a few flowers per plant to ripen into seed. Lemon balm forms its small flowers close to the stem, so it's not practical to remove individual blooms. In this case, the easiest approach to deadheading is to shear all the stems back by one-half to two-thirds a week or so after you first see the flowers open. Leave one or two stems uncut on each plant for seed production. And on the lady's mantle, clip the flowering stems off at the base of the plant.

Angelica

While this garden starts with a plan, be prepared for it to change over time as the plants mature or move around. As the rose grows, for instance, it will eventually shade out the chives, lady's mantle, and dill growing near its base. But by that time, they'll have seeded into sunnier spots, so you'll still be able to enjoy them!

Lady's mantle

CARE THROUGH THE SEASONS

This herbal flower garden is ideal for a full-sun site with average, well-drained soil. If possible, set out the perennial herbs in early to midspring or late summer to early fall. Summer planting is okay, too, but you'll need to pay close attention to watering new plantings during this season.

Early to midspring. If you decide to start this garden in spring, you can set out the perennials and rose as soon you get them.

In following years, use this time to clean up any debris that has gathered in the garden. Pull out chickweed and other cool-season weeds and remove any winter-killed growth on the angelica, chives, lady's mantle, and lemon balm. Once new growth emerges on the hyssop and rue, trim off any dead shoots; then cut the remaining stems back by one-half to two-thirds of their total length to shape the plant. (Make the cuts just above an emerging leaf or leaf pair.)

Early spring is the time to prune your sweet briar rose. Trim out all dead growth and then cut out two or three of the oldest stems.

Once you finish the cleanup and pruning, rake off the loose mulch and pile it at the side of the garden. Spread a ½-inch layer of compost over the soil (try not to pile it on the crowns of the perennials), or scatter all-purpose organic fertilizer over the soil according to the recommended application rates. Replace the old mulch and add more if needed to maintain a 2-inch layer.

Each spring, sow the seed of the annuals (calendulas and dill) directly in the garden. (Dill is particularly fussy about transplanting, so it really grows best when it's direct-sown.) Pull aside the mulch to expose the soil in the allotted areas; then scatter the seed evenly over the spaces. Press the dill seed lightly into the soil surface or cover it with a sprinkling of soil. Cover the calendula seed with ¼ inch of soil. Keep the area evenly moist until seedlings appear. Both dill and calendula readily self-sow in many areas. So you may not need to do much, if any, new seeding of these plants.

Calendula

Midspring to midsummer. Once the calendula and dill seedlings are a few inches tall, thin them to stand about 6 inches apart. Pull the mulch back around them, but don't pile it right against their stems.

Dill

If you didn't direct-sow the calendula seeds in spring, set out transplants around your last frost date. (Not sure of the last frost date in your area? Ask other gardeners in your neighborhood or check with your local garden center or Cooperative Extension Service.)

After all your herbs are in the ground, there's not much to do: Just pull out any weeds while they are still small. During dry spells, water new plantings as needed to keep the soil evenly moist. Established herbs can tolerate dry conditions, so there's no need to water them unless rainfall is lacking and the top 2 or 3 inches of soil are dry under the mulch.

Midsummer to midfall. Regular deadheading is a must to keep your cottage garden herbs looking their best and to minimize self-sowing. For specific tips, see Problem Prevention on page 61. Don't deadhead the rose, though, or it won't bear those beautiful red fruits.

If hot weather causes your calendulas to stop blooming, try cutting them back to 3 inches above the soil (they may resprout and rebloom) or pull them out and sow more seed for a flush of flowers in the fall. Other than that, just water, weed, and add more mulch if needed to maintain the 2-inch layer.

Midfall through winter. Keep deadheading regularly, but remember to leave a few flowers on each plant if you want some self-sown seedlings next year. Both calendulas and dill can tolerate some frost, so leave them in place until after a heavy freeze.

During the first winter, consider protecting your new planting with a generous layer of loose straw or evergreen boughs, especially if you live in an area where snow cover is not reliable. Make sure you wait until the soil is frozen before you mulch; otherwise, you might encourage voles or other critters to make their winter home in your garden.

A FRIENDLY FRONT-DOOR GARDEN

When you're looking for another place to add herbs to your yard, don't forget the front of your house. What could be more welcoming to your visitors than a fragrant, flower-filled herb garden near your front door? Replace those boring evergreen shrubs with this cheerful combination of colorful foliage and long-lasting flowers, a wonderful way to invite friends and family into your home.

With a high-visibility site like this, it's important to choose plants that look good all season long — and even through winter, if possible. One way to extend the interest is by selecting plants that bloom for at least a month or longer. It just makes sense to get the most flower power possible in this important space.

Foliage also plays a critical role in keeping your front-door garden looking great from spring through fall. This garden, for instance, includes the lacy, fernlike foliage of yarrow and Roman chamomile, which makes a handsome contrast to the broad shape of many other leaves. If the foliage has a pleasant scent, that's a plus. Whether it's the fruity scent of a chamomile leaf trodden underfoot; the warm, pungent aroma of culinary sage; or the licorice-like fragrance of fennel, your visitors will remember the pleasing scents that linger around your door.

Most of all, though, it's important to search out plants that have colorful foliage. You'll be looking at the leaves from early spring well into fall, so try to get as much color as you can. Herbs are especially generous in offering many great colored-foliage selections, such as yellow-green golden oregano, chocolate-brown bronze fennel, and purple-green purple sage.

Choose plants with winter interest, and you have a truly year-round garden. The large red fruits of rugosa rose, for instance, are an excellent addition, since they provide color and interest well into the depths of the off-season. Sages tend to hold some of their foliage well into winter, while golden feverfew, golden oregano, and Roman chamomile all keep some ground-hugging-but-still-visible top growth through most winters. Put these all together, and you have a winning combination for a fabulous front-door garden!

Friendly Front-Door Garden

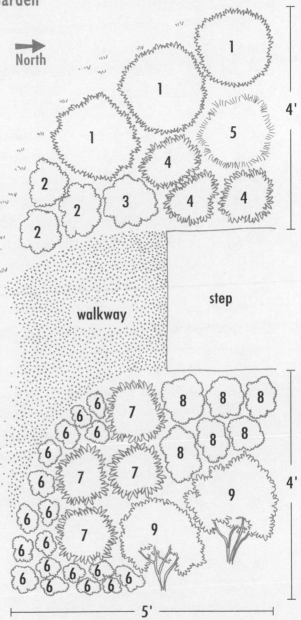

North

PLANT LIST

1. Anise hyssop *(Agastache foeniculum)*, 3*
2. Golden oregano (*Origanum vulgare* 'Aureum'), 3
3. 'Appleblossom' yarrow (*Achillea millefolium* 'Appleblossom'), 1
4. Variegated sage (*Salvia officinalis* 'Icterina'), 3
5. Bronze fennel (*Foeniculum vulgare* 'Purpureum'), 1
6. Roman chamomile (*Chamaemelum nobile*), 18
7. Purple sage (*Salvia officinalis* 'Purpurea'), 4
8. Golden feverfew (*Tanacetum parthenium* 'Aureum'), 6
9. Rugosa rose *(Rosa rugosa)*, 2

*The number after the botanical name indicates the number of plants needed.

CUSTOMIZING THIS DESIGN

Most of the plants in this design are dependably cold-hardy through Zone 5, so this garden would suit a sunny, well-drained site in many areas. Here are some ideas to help customize the design to fit your personal tastes.

Other foliage options. Looking for additional options in good-looking foliage for all-season interest? Consider adding a variety of silver-leaved plants to your garden, in the form of artemisias, lavenders, 'Berggarten' sage, lavender cotton, or 'Silver Shield' sorrel. Rue leaves also have a beautiful blue-gray cast, and the cultivar 'Variegata' offers white-streaked or even all-white leaves.

Rue

Rosy thoughts. If you're wondering why this design calls for two rose plants, it's because rugosa roses benefit from cross-pollination to produce their beautiful red fruits (known as hips). In a small space, you may not have room for two separate bushes, but if you plant them next to each other, you'll have a full-looking shrub with lots of flowers and plenty of pretty hips. If you'd rather choose a rose that doesn't need cross-pollination to set fruit, you'll need only one plant. Check pot labels or catalog descriptions to find selections that have handsome fruits. Pink-flowered 'Carefree Beauty' is one widely available, disease-resistant cultivar that produces good-looking, orange-red hips.

PROBLEM PREVENTION

This easy-care garden should seldom present any problems. Even the recommended rose — rugosa rose — is tough enough to resist most of the pests and diseases that bother its relatives. The only problem you might see is rose stem girdler. The adults are small green beetles that lay eggs under the bark. The eggs hatch into grubs that feed on the stems, causing the bark to swell and split. If you notice these symptoms, prune out the infested canes and destroy them.

CARE THROUGH THE SEASONS

This entrance garden is best suited to a sunny site with average, well-drained soil. You can get it started just about any time of year, as long as the ground isn't frozen and the plants are available. In most areas, though, the best planting times are early to midspring and late summer to early fall, times when cool air and ample moisture encourage good root growth.

Early to midspring. If you're starting your garden in spring, set out the perennials and roses as soon as you get them. After planting, water thoroughly and then add a 2-inch layer of an organic mulch, such as chopped leaves. Make sure you leave a 2- to 4-inch-diameter mulch-free zone at the base of each plant so the mulch isn't piled against the stems.

In established gardens, start the spring cleanup by clipping off any dead stems from the anise hyssop, chamomile, fennel, feverfew, oregano, and yarrow. Be careful not to damage the new growth emerging from the base of the plants. Also, pull out any early weeds that have emerged.

Your roses will benefit from some yearly attention in late winter or early spring. First, prune out any dead stems; then remove one-third of the oldest stems at ground level. Trim the remaining stems by one-third of their total length, making each cut a little above an outward-facing bud.

Once you're finished with cleanup and pruning, rake off the loose mulch. Spread a ½-inch layer of compost over the whole garden (try not to pile it on the crowns of the perennials), or scatter all-purpose organic fertilizer over the soil, following the application rate suggested on the package. Replace the material you raked off and add fresh mulch if needed to keep the layer 2 inches thick.

Midspring to midsummer. During dry spells, water new plantings as needed to keep the soil evenly moist. Well-established herbs can tolerate dry conditions, however, so there's no need to water them unless rainfall is lacking and the top 2 or 3 inches of soil are dry under the mulch.

Midsummer to midfall. Removing spent flowers regularly will help keep your front-door garden looking good for months. Cut yarrow stems to the ground when their blooms fade and clip off spent anise hyssop blooms just above the uppermost set of leaves. Clip off the bronze fennel's flower clusters as soon as the yellow flowers fade. (Both the anise hyssop and fennel will produce many seedlings unless you deadhead regularly.) On the golden feverfew, you can pinch off individual blooms, but it's easier to shear whole plants back to about 3 inches above the ground after their first flush of bloom. If your golden oregano plants sprawl after they flower, leaving an open center, trim them back by one-half to two-thirds to promote a flush of bushier new growth. Remember not to dead-head the rose, so you can enjoy its scarlet hips. Other than that, just keep weeding and watering as needed.

Bronze fennel

Midfall through winter. Continue deadheading your herbs as needed. Some people like to let the last blooms stay on their anise hyssop plants for winter interest. While I'm all for winter interest, I've made the mistake of letting my anise hyssop plants set seed too often and then ended up pulling up the resulting seedlings by the handful. If you do choose to leave some seed heads, pay special attention to maintaining the mulch layer around the plants. I've found that an extrathick layer of mulch (3 or 4 inches) keeps anise hyssop seeds from reaching the soil, and the seeds that do sprout are easier to pull out of the fluffy mulch layer.

Throughout the winter, check the garden every week or two (especially after a warm spell) to make sure the freezing and thawing isn't pushing plants out of the soil. If you do see frost-heaved plants, cover the exposed roots with mulch or soil to keep them from drying out. In early spring, dig up the heaved plants and reset them at the proper planting depth.

CHAPTER 3

ESSENTIAL
Landscape Herbs
A to Z

Great gardens start with great plants! In this chapter, you'll learn about some of the many beautiful annual and perennial herbs you can use in all parts of your landscape. I've included over 30 of my favorites, and there are many more species and selections that I didn't have room for. The herbs covered here represent some of the most versatile and dependable choices for getting a garden started.

In each entry, you'll learn the basics of selecting, growing, and propagating that particular plant, as well as advice on ways to use the herb in your landscape. I've also included some suggestions of combinations you can create with each herb. Try them as is, or use them as inspiration for making your own beautiful plant pairings!

AGASTACHES

Known as: Anise hyssop, licorice mint *(Agastache foeniculum)*, Korean mint *(A. rugosa)*

Plant type: Perennial

Licorice or root beer? Their exact fragrance may be hard to describe, but it's definitely not hard to find a place for these handsome perennial herbs in a sunny garden. As a plus, agastaches are as attractive to butterflies as they are to gardeners.

Anise hyssop

What they look like. You can tell agastaches are mint-family members by their square stems and aromatic leaves, which are opposite each other on the stems. These bushy plants produce small, tubular flowers in dense or open spikes during the summer. The foliage may be broad or narrow and green or gray-green, depending on the species.

Which one to choose. You might not find agastaches at your local garden center, but herb growers usually carry at least one species. The most commonly available species is anise hyssop *(Agastache foeniculum)*. This North American native blooms from midsummer into fall with dense spikes of light purple flowers. All parts of the 2- to 3-foot plants are strongly aromatic. 'Alabaster' has white flowers. 'Fragrant Delight' is a seed strain that produces light purple, pink, or white flowers.

Native to eastern Asia, Korean mint *(A. rugosa)* looks much like anise hyssop but is usually taller, reaching 3 to 4 feet in height. Both anise hyssop and Korean mint are usually hardy in Zones 5 to 9.

A. rupestris is a southwest United States native with small, gray-green, roughly triangular leaves and loose spikes of pinkish orange flowers from summer into fall. You might also run across a few more unusual species or hybrids in specialty herb catalogs. 'Apricot Sunrise' is similar to *A. rupestris* but with narrower leaves and apricot-orange flowers; 'Toronjil Morado' has pink flowers. As you read catalog descriptions, you'll find a wide variety of hardiness ranges given for these agastaches. Some sources say they are hardy only in frost-free areas; others claim they're hardy as far north as Zone 5! I've had *A. rupestris* and 'Apricot Sunrise' overwinter in my mid–Zone 6 garden, so I encourage you to experiment.

Where to plant them. Agastaches thrive in full sun, but they'll also tolerate light shade. Average, well-drained soil suits most of them. Anise hyssop and Korean mint can adapt to moist sites, but they are also drought tolerant once established. With *A. rupestris* and some of the other agastaches that are questionably hardy, excellent drainage can help improve the chances of successful overwintering outdoors.

How to grow them. These easy-care herbs don't need much maintenance. Anise hyssop and Korean mint can self-sow prolifically, though, so I suggest regular deadheading to keep them from getting weedy. (Keeping a thick layer of mulch around the plants is another option.) Do let a few flowers set seed, though; agastaches can be short-lived, so it's good to have a few replacements coming along.

Most agastaches are easy to grow from seed sown indoors in early to midspring. They'll germinate in about a week at 70°F and usually bloom the first year. Space plants about 2 feet apart. All agastaches also root quickly from summer stem cuttings, and that's the easiest way to propagate the hybrids. (See Making More Herbs on page 144 for information on propagating by cuttings.)

How to use them. Agastaches are excellent choices for the middle or back of a bed or border. With their dense, bushy growth, anise hyssop and Korean mint also make great summer hedges. Agastaches are popular with birds, bees, and butterflies but are said to be deer resistant. The blooms make great cut flowers.

What to plant with them. Adaptable agastaches combine well with a wide range of sun-loving annuals and perennials. The spiky bloom clusters look especially good with daisylike or rounded blooms, such as those of purple coneflower and yarrow. (This grouping makes a great foundation for a butterfly garden, by the way.)

ANGELICAS

Known as: Archangel, garden angelica, wild parsnip *(Angelica archangelica)*

Plant type: Perennial

Angelicas are the giants of the herb garden. It's hard to miss these imposing perennials when they're in full bloom!

Angelica

What they look like. Angelicas start out as a 2- to 3-foot-wide rosette of large, bright green, irregularly toothed leaves that look much like celery foliage. After a year or two (or three), the clumps are large enough to send up 4- to 8-foot-tall, hollow stems topped with domed clusters of many tiny flowers in midsummer. Angelicas generally die after they set seed in late summer.

Which one to choose. The most commonly grown angelica is known botanically as *Angelica archangelica*. This species has greenish white flowers. A more recent addition to our angelica options is *A. gigas,* with purple stems, purple-flushed leaves, and reddish purple flower buds opening to tiny white flowers.

If you're looking for something really different, check seed-exchange lists or specialty nurseries for *A. pachycarpa,* also listed as *A. pachyfolia* and *A. japonica.* In my experience, seed obtained under any of these names produces much more compact plants — to about 3 feet tall when in bloom — with greenish white flowers. Besides being easier to squeeze into a small garden, these plants offer beautiful dark green leaves that have an eye-catching shiny coating. All of these angelicas are hardy in Zones 4 to 8.

Where to plant them. Angelicas appreciate evenly moist soil that's been enriched with organic matter. Partial shade is best in most areas, especially where summers are hot; in cool-summer areas, angelicas can grow well in full sun.

How to grow them. These easy-care herbs don't need much maintenance to look their best, although they do appreciate a generous helping of compost mulch each spring. When they flower, you have two options: Let the seeds form and drop to produce new plants, or cut off the flower stems near the base of the plant as the blooms begin to fade. Removing the spent flower stems regularly can extend the life of your original plant for several years, since this encourages the plant to put its energy toward root production.

If you need only one clump of angelica — and many gardens don't have room for more than that — it's easiest to start with a purchased plant. To get more plants, simply let the original clump self-sow; then dig and move the seedlings to where you want them while they are small. Or collect the seeds, then sow them outdoors where you want them to grow, or in a nursery bed or a pot, in fall or early spring. Don't cover the seeds; just press them into the soil surface and keep it moist until seedlings appear. Thin or transplant seedlings to stand 3 to 4 feet apart.

How to use them. These statuesque herbs are a natural choice when you need an accent plant at the back or end of a border. They also look handsome planted in a row along a fence or wall.

What to plant with them. Angelicas look great with other plants that appreciate cool, moist conditions, such as calendulas, lemon balm, and nasturtiums.

ARTEMISIAS

Known as: Silver sage *(Artemisia ludoviciana),* southernwood *(A. abrotanum),* white mugwort *(A. lactiflora),* wormwood *(A. absinthium)*

Plant type: Perennial

Artemisias are an indispensable addition to sunny gardens, since their silvery foliage makes a perfect complement to other herbs, setting off their colors. Their pungent aroma is another plus.

Silver
sage

What they look like. Artemisias generally grow as dense, shrubby clumps, often with somewhat woody stems. Except in one species, artemisia flowers tend to be small and yellow-green, so don't count on them for fabulous blooms. Their main claim to fame is their foliage, which is usually aromatic and covered with silvery hairs.

Which one to choose. 'Powis Castle' is a popular hybrid and rightly so: It produces large, nonspreading, shrubby mounds of finely cut, silvery white leaves. Generally hardy in Zones 5 to 8, it grows 2 to 3 feet tall and 3 to 4 feet wide. Wormwood *(A. absinthium)*, one of the parents of 'Powis Castle', is similar but with gray-green foliage from a semi-woody base; it grows 3 to 4 feet tall. This herb-garden classic is also hardier, growing in Zones 3 to 8.

Cultivars of silver sage *(A. ludoviciana)* are popular for creating herbal wreaths. All have jagged-edged, silvery leaves on nonwoody stems. 'Silver King', with its very narrow leaves, is the most widely grown. 'Silver Queen' is very similar but with somewhat wider foliage. Both grow 2 to 3 feet tall and are hardy in Zones 4 to 8. 'Valerie Finnis' is a newer introduction, with even wider leaves in tidy 18- to 36-inch mounds. Hardy in Zones 4 to 9, it is becoming popular with southern gardeners, since it is more tolerant of heat and humidity.

My favorite artemisia is southernwood *(A. abrotanum)*, with nearly threadlike leaves on woody stems that produce handsome domed clumps 2 to 3 feet tall and wide. Its scent is a little odd at first, and some people don't like it, but give it a chance — it will grow on you! Camphor-scented southernwood *(A. abrotanum* var. *camphorata)* seems to be the most widely available variety. It has wispy, silvery green leaves and usually grows 2 to 3 feet tall. The gray-green foliage of lemon-scented southernwood *(A. abrotanum* var. *limoneum)* has more of a lemony scent. This variety grows 3 to 4 feet tall. Tangerine-scented southernwood *(A. abrotanum* var. *procera)* is the tallest type, with greener leaves

Southernwood

on woody, strongly upright stems reaching to 5 feet tall. All three varieties are hardy in Zones 5 to 9.

Unlike its relatives, white mugwort *(A. lactiflora)* offers interesting creamy white, lightly fragrant flowers, borne in showy plumes in late summer or early fall. They bloom atop 4- to 6-foot stems clad in finely cut green leaves with white undersides. 'Guizho' is similar but has dark purple stems and purple-green leaves. Both are hardy in Zones 4 to 9.

Where to plant them. Most artemisias thrive in full sun and well-drained to dry soil. White mugwort is an exception, preferring moist soil, but it actually produces stronger, more compact stems in drier conditions. Give the spreading types — especially white mugwort and silver sage — a spot where they can creep freely or plant them within a barrier.

Mugwort

How to grow them. Space artemisias about 2 feet apart. Woody-stemmed artemisias benefit from regular trimming. In late spring, once new growth has appeared, trim the stems back by one-third to one-half, making cuts just above emerging buds. Trim again lightly in summer to shape plants or to encourage new bushy growth if the stems flop. Propagate these woody-stemmed plants in late summer by taking stem cuttings, ideally with a bit of old wood at the base of each.

Shear nonwoody artemisias back by one-half to two-thirds in late spring to early summer. Divide plants every two to three years in spring or fall for propagation or to control their spread.

How to use them. Silver-leaved artemisias blend beautifully with other colors of foliage and flowers. They are also a perfect addition to white gardens, where the plumy flowers of white mugwort are also an asset. The dense, shrubby habit of the woody-stemmed types makes them ideal for summer hedges.

What to plant with them. Pair artemisias with lavenders, santolinas, and other herbs that thrive in full sun and well-drained soil. Including plants with green, gold, or purple foliage will provide some contrast. Southernwood planted under roses is a classic combination.

BASILS

Known as: Sweet basil *(Ocimum basilicum)*

Plant type: Annual

These versatile herbs are as ornamental as they are tasty. Tall or small, green or purple, smooth or crinkled — there's a basil for practically every purpose!

Lemon basil

What they look like. Like other Mint Family members, basils have square stems and aromatic, opposite leaves. All produce spikes of white or pinkish flowers. Beyond that, though, these annual herbs vary widely in heights, habits, and fragrance.

Which one to choose. The real challenge in growing basil is deciding which to try! The classic culinary choice is sweet basil *(Ocimum basilicum)*, with wrinkled, glossy, bright green leaves that have a spicy scent and flavor. The fast-growing, branching stems can reach 30 inches in height. 'Mammoth' is a selection with much larger leaves. In contrast, 'Spicy Globe' has small leaves that grow in tight, dense mounds about 16 inches tall and wide. 'Spicy Globe' seedlings can vary somewhat in leaf size and shape. 'Minette' is a seed strain that produces more uniform plants.

Cinnamon basil

Looking for interesting leaves? 'Green Ruffles' is a selection of sweet basil grown for its large, crinkly green leaves. 'Purple Ruffles', as you might expect, is similar, except that its foliage is a deep purple color. 'Red Rubin' has smooth-textured, reddish purple foliage.

In the unusual-flavor department, the maroon-flushed stems and leaves of 'Anise' have a light licorice scent and flavor. 'Cinnamon' looks similar but has the scent and flavor of cinnamon. Lemon basil *(O. basilicum citriodorum)* has small, pointed, bright green leaves with a distinct lemon scent and flavor. 'Mrs. Burns' is a more vigorous selection of lemon basil.

Among the many other beautiful basils, 'African Blue' is one of my favorites, with purple stems and aromatic, purple-veined leaves on 3-foot plants. This hybrid doesn't seem to set seed, and I let it bloom so I can enjoy the long spikes of light purple flowers. You can keep this one from year to year by potting it up before frost and putting it on a sunny, warm windowsill for the winter.

Where to plant them. Basils need full sun and warm, well-drained soil. Raised beds are ideal because they promote good drainage and warm up quickly in the spring. Remember that while basils don't like soggy soil, they do like a steady supply of moisture.

'Purple Ruffles' basil

How to grow them. Basils don't ask for much: just lots of light, ample moisture, and warm conditions. Mulch helps keep the soil evenly moist and prevents soil from splashing up on the leaves. To encourage more leafy growth, regularly pinch off the flower buds as soon as they begin to emerge.

Basil is easy to grow from seed. Sow directly in the garden in mid- to late spring, cover with a sprinkling of soil, and keep evenly moist; the seed will germinate as soon as warm conditions arrive. For an earlier start, sow seed indoors in early to midspring and cover with ⅛ inch of seed-starting mix. At 70°F, seedlings should appear in one to two weeks. When seedlings have at least two pairs of true leaves, transplant them to individual pots. (After seed germination, true leaves are those that follow the first pair of leaves to appear, generally called *seed leaves*.) Set out transplants after all danger of frost has passed, spacing them 8 to 12 inches apart.

How to use them. These beautiful and fragrant herbs deserve a place in all parts of your landscape. The purple-leaved basils are particularly pretty planted in beds, borders, and containers.

What to plant with them. Basils blend well with other annuals and perennials that appreciate evenly moist soil. Purple-leaved basils combine beautifully with red, pink, orange, and yellow flowers and make a great contrast to golden foliage.

BEE BALMS

Known as: Bee balm *(Monarda didyma)*, horsemint *(M. punctata)*, lemon mint *(M. citriodora)*

Plant type: Varies by species

Bee balm

Bee balms' shaggy-looking blooms are a stunning sight in the summer garden. As a plus, the bees and hummingbirds that visit your garden will enjoy these flowers just as much as you do.

What they look like. Square stems, opposite leaves, and a spreading habit indicate that these perennial or annual herbs are part of the mint family. Through the summer, they produce tubular florets that are arranged in whorls at or near the tips of the stems. All parts of the plant are fragrant.

Which one to choose. Most of the widely grown bee balms are selections of *Monarda didyma* or hybrids with other species. 'Gardenview Scarlet' is a commonly available red-flowered cultivar that's highly promoted for its resistance to powdery mildew, a common fungal disease, but plants I've grown under that name tend to get some mildew each year. I have much better luck with 'Jacob Cline', a selection with huge heads of bright red flowers. 'Scorpio' offers violet-purple flowers; 'Snow White' has white flowers (both of these have moderate disease resistance). Hybrid 'Marshall's Delight' is one of my favorites, with dense heads of bright pink flowers and excellent mildew resistance. The above selections all grow 3 to 4 feet tall. If you need a shorter plant, try 'Petite Delight', with rosy pink flowers on 12- to 18-inch plants. All of these grow best in Zones 5 to 8, but you can often have luck in one zone warmer or cooler.

Horsemint *(M. punctata)* is a hairy, short-lived perennial with 2- to 3-foot stems that bear whorls of purple-spotted yellow blooms over rosy pink bracts along the upper portions of the stems. Horsemint is hardy in Zones 5 to 9.

Lemon mint *(M. citriodora)*, an annual species, produces bushy plants with whorls of lavender-pink flowers along the upper parts of its 1- to 3-foot stems.

Where to plant them. Bee balms generally thrive in full sun and evenly moist, well-drained soil. (Horsemint prefers drier conditions.) Bee balms can take light shade and may bloom a bit longer there, but their stems may be weaker and might need staking.

How to grow them. Regular deadheading can help prolong bloom. After a few years, clumps may die out in the center. Divide every two to three years in spring, replanting only the vigorous outer portions of the clump. Division is also the easiest way to propagate the perennial bee balms. Propagate horsemint and lemon mint by sowing seed indoors or outdoors in early spring. Seedlings will appear in about two weeks at 70°F. Space perennial bee balms about 2 feet apart. For lemon mint, thin seedlings or set transplants 8 to 12 inches apart.

How to use them. Bee balms are ideal for informal gardens, but they can also look great in formal borders, if you're willing to divide them regularly to control their spread. These beauties are indispensable for attracting bees, hummingbirds, and butterflies to any garden.

What to plant with them. Combine bee balms with other vigorous plants, such as agastaches, yarrows, and ornamental grasses. All of the colors look great paired with the yellow foliage of 'All Gold' lemon balm.

Avoiding Mildew

Many bee balms are susceptible to powdery mildew, a fungal disease that causes dusty gray patches on foliage and flowers and may lead to leaf drop. Avoid this by choosing mildew-resistant cultivars. If mildew still appears, cut down all the stems to the new growth emerging at ground level. The following spring, divide the clump or cut out about one-third of the stems at ground level to allow good air circulation around foliage.

CALENDULA

Known as: Calendula, pot marigold
(*Calendula officinalis*)

Plant type: Annual

Calendula
Calendula's bright orange or yellow blooms bring a touch of sunny cheer to any early summer garden. This cool-season annual tends to fade out in the heat of midsummer, but with a bit of care, you can invite it back for a fall performance.

What it looks like. Calendula plants are generally compact and bushy at the base, with green, spatula-shaped leaves. Their real claim to fame is their single or double daisylike flowers, which range in color from dark orange to pale yellow and bloom atop wiry stems up to 2 feet tall. The flowers tend to close at night and on cloudy days.

Which one to choose. 'Pacific Beauty' is a classic cultivar with double flowers in a range of oranges and yellows on 18- to 24-inch stems. 'Fiesta Gitana' produces similar flowers on compact, 1-foot plants. The flowers of 'Kablouna Yellow' are rather different from most, with a ring of outer petals surrounding a domed center of tightly packed petals. The clear yellow flowers bloom on 18- to 24-inch stems. My all-time favorite is 18-inch-tall 'Touch of Red Mixed': The back of each petal has a maroon blush, giving the "touch of red" effect to the top cream, orange, or yellow color.

Where to plant it. These no-fail annuals thrive in sun or light shade. They grow well in average to rich, well-drained soil.

How to grow it. If you want an extra-early start, sow calendula seeds indoors in early spring and cover with ¼ inch of seed-starting mix. Seedlings should appear in one to two weeks at 70°F. Calendulas grow so readily from seed, however, that it's just as easy to sow them directly in the garden. Sow in early fall or very early spring in the south. In the north, direct-sow in early spring and, if your summers are cool, again in early summer for fall flowers. Thin seedlings or set transplants 8 to 12 inches apart.

Deadhead regularly to prolong the bloom season. Maintain a generous mulch layer and water regularly to keep the soil cool and moist. If plants start to decline due to summer heat, try cutting them back to about 3 inches above the ground; they may produce a new flush of leaves and flowers. If you don't see any regrowth in a week or two, pull out the plants and try sowing again for a fall display.

How to use it. Full-sized calendulas are cheerful additions to cottage gardens and informal plantings. Compact cultivars can make cute edgings for beds and borders and also look great in containers.

What to plant with it. Bright orange and yellow calendulas pair perfectly with other intensely colored flowers, such as red petunias, blue edging lobelia *(Lobelia erinus),* and the jewel-tone hues of many nasturtiums. I particularly like the contrast of calendulas against the blue-green foliage of rue.

Count Your Chickens

For a real novelty, try hen-and-chickens marigold *(Calendula officinalis* var. *prolifera).* A ring of short stems emerges from the base of each typical double flower, producing a circle of smaller daisies that bloom slightly above the main flower.

CATMINTS

Known as: Catmint *(Nepeta × faassenii* and *N. mussinii),* catnip *(N. cataria),* Siberian catmint *(N. sibirica)*

Plant type: Perennial species

These old-fashioned favorites aren't just popular with cats — they're beloved by generations of gardeners as well. And with their classic combination of purple-blue flowers and gray-green foliage, it's little wonder catmints are a must-have for many herb lovers.

Catmint

What they look like. Like their cousins, the true mints, catmints have opposite, aromatic leaves on square stems. The green or gray-green leaves are roughly heart shaped. Typically blue-purple in color, the tubular flowers bloom in whorls along the stem tips.

Which one to choose. Don't get confused between catmint and catnip. Catnip *(Nepeta cataria)* is the one that's a hit with kitties. While it's not showy, with white to pinkish, mid- to late-summer flowers and fuzzy gray leaves on 3-foot stems, it's been grown for centuries for its medicinal qualities. Lemon catnip (*N. cataria* 'Citriodora') has an aroma that is supposedly more appealing to people and less attractive to cats. Catnip is hardy in Zones 3 to 8.

Catnip

Among the more ornamental catmints, there is some confusion about correct names. The most widely grown seems to be Faassen's catmint *(N. × faassenii),* but you'll also see many cultivars listed as belonging to *N. mussinii,* or with no species name at all. 'Blue Wonder' is a popular selection with lavender-blue summer flowers and gray-green foliage on 12- to 15-inch plants. 'White Wonder' is a white-flowered version. 'Walker's Low' is even more compact (usually 10 to 12 inches), with lavender-blue flowers. On the other size extreme, 'Six Hills Giant' has deep purple-blue blooms on plants that reach 3 feet tall and wide. 'Dropmore' grows 18 inches tall with bright purple-blue flowers. 'Souvenir D'Andre Chaudron' is a selection of Siberian catmint *(N. sibirica)* with large purple-blue flowers and green foliage on 2- to 3-foot plants. For something different, try 'Dawn to Dusk', with sprays of soft pink blooms from summer into fall. The 2- to 3-foot stems form mounds of gray-green leaves. All of these selections are generally hardy in Zones 4 to 8.

Where to plant them. Grow catmints in full sun to light shade. These sturdy perennials perform best in average to dry, well-drained soil; moist, fertile conditions can cause weak, sprawling stems.

How to grow them. After flowering, shear catmints back to remove the spent blooms, minimize reseeding, and encourage new leafy growth and possible rebloom. Propagate catmints by dividing clumps or digging up and transplanting rooted stems in spring, or take cuttings in early summer. Space compact cultivars 1 foot apart; allow at least 18 to 24 inches between medium- and large-growing catmints.

How to use them. Low-growing catmints make great ground covers, and they also look wonderful as an edging for flower gardens. Site the taller varieties at the middle or back of beds and borders.

What to plant with them. Enjoy these easy-to-grow perennials with other dependable bloomers, such as feverfew, purple coneflowers, and yarrows. Catmints are a classic companion for planting under roses.

CHAMOMILES

Known as: German chamomile *(Matricaria recutita),* Roman chamomile *(Chamaemelum nobile)*

Plant type: German chamomile — annual; Roman chamomile — perennial

These charming herbs produce clumps or carpets of ferny green foliage sprinkled with delightful little white daisies. They look dainty, but they are generally trouble-free and easy to grow in a sunny spot.

Roman chamomile

What they look like. Chamomiles bear finely cut, bright green leaves and yellow-centered, white-petaled daisies.

Which one to choose. German chamomile *(Matricaria recutita)* is an annual plant that produces upright, many-branched clumps of feathery foliage growing about 18 inches tall. Each plant produces dozens of single white daisies. Roman chamomile *(Chamaemelum nobile)* is a perennial, and it is much more compact; it also produces fewer flowers per plant. Its dense rosettes of finely cut, fragrant leaves grow together to form thick carpets usually less than 4 inches tall. The flower stems reach 6 to 8 inches tall. Regular Roman chamomile has single white daisies. 'Flore Pleno' has creamy white, double flowers. 'Treneague' does not flower so it makes a neater ground cover, but it seems to grow more slowly and be more prone to winter damage than other Roman chamomiles. Roman chamomile grows best in Zones 6 to 8.

Where to plant them. Both chamomiles grow well in average, well-drained soil. They generally thrive in full sun but appreciate midday shade in hot, dry climates.

How to grow them. Pull out German chamomile plants when they decline after bloom. Shear off the spent flower stems of Roman chamomile just above the foliage.

German chamomile

Sow German chamomile seed outdoors in early spring, scattering the seed as evenly as possible. (Mixing the seed with a few spoonfuls of clean sand can make it easier to spread the seed evenly.) Sowing again in summer will give you a later-season show.

Roman chamomile grows easily from seed sown indoors in early spring. Don't cover the seed. Look for seedlings in one to two weeks at 70°F. Set out transplants about 8 inches apart around the last frost date.

How to use them. Use German chamomile to add color and interest to flower gardens. It is especially good for filling around newly planted perennials for the first year or two.

Roman chamomile makes a great ground cover for a sunny spot. It's soft and springy underfoot and releases its sweet scent when stepped on. It can't tolerate much foot traffic, however, so make sure you add stepping-stones if you need access into the area. Roman chamomile also looks great as an edging for container plantings.

What to plant with them. Chamomiles' dainty white daisies are sweetly appealing with other white or yellow flowers, such as those of pale yellow 'Moonlight' nasturtiums. Purple or blue flowers also make a nice contrast, so try chamomiles with hyssop or lavenders. Create a cheerful picture by planting chamomiles next to herbs with handsome foliage, such as the glossy green leaves of germander or the yellow-and-green leaves of golden sage.

CHIVES

Known as: Common chives *(Allium schoenoprasum)*, garlic chives *(A. tuberosum)*

Plant type: Perennial

Sure, they're great on baked potatoes, but chives also have a lot to offer in the ornamental department. Their clusters of pink or white flowers are their main claim to fame, but the grasslike foliage also makes an interesting textural statement.

Chives

What they look like. These perennial herbs produce clumps of long, narrow, smooth leaves that emerge bright green and age to dark green. The early to midsummer flowers bloom in attractive, rounded clusters.

Which one to choose. You're probably already familiar with common chives *(Allium schoenoprasum)*. This culinary classic grows in clumps usually 12 to 18 inches tall, with cylindrical, hollow leaves and pink to purplish flowers in late spring to early summer. Both the leaves and flowers have a mild onion flavor. 'Forescate' is a selection with larger flower clusters that are definitely on the rosy pink side. Common chives are hardy in Zones 4 to 8.

Another worthwhile species to try is garlic chives *(A. tuberosum)*. Its garlic-flavored green leaves are flat and solid, but the 18- to 24-inch clumps still have an overall grassy look. Garlic chives bloom two or three months later than common chives, lighting up the late-summer garden with clusters of sweetly scented white flowers. This handsome herb is hardy in Zones 4 to 8.

Garlic chives

Where to plant them. Both kinds of chives grow fine in average, well-drained soil. They prefer full sun but can take light shade; in fact, they seem to appreciate midday shade (and evenly moist soil) in hot-summer climates.

How to grow them. These easy herbs don't take much maintenance. Your main job will be to remove the spent flower heads regularly; otherwise, you'll have chive seedlings everywhere!

Considering how readily chives reproduce on their own, it's not surprising that it's easy to start them from seed. Sow in 2- to 3-inch pots indoors in early spring, scattering a pinch of seed evenly over the top of each pot, and cover with ¼ inch of seed-starting mix. Look for seedlings in a week or two at 70°F. Transplant seedlings outdoors after the last frost date, moving the entire potful as one clump. Space clumps 8 to 12 inches apart. Keep established clumps vigorous by dividing them every three to five years in spring; replant only the outer portions.

How to use them. The handsome clumps of grassy foliage make chives an excellent choice for edging beds and borders. Think twice about planting them close to pathways, though, unless you don't mind their oniony fragrance when you brush by or step on the leaves.

What to plant with them. Attractive growing under roses for an early summer show, common chives also pair well with many other flowering herbs, including catmints and feverfew. Golden-foliaged herbs are especially wonderful companions; one of my favorite combinations is common chives with 'All Gold' lemon balm. Garlic chives' white flowers blend beautifully with the blue foliage of rue. For more of a contrast, try the dark green leaves of germander or the chocolate-brown foliage of bronze fennel. Both kinds of chives look great in front of silvery foliage, such as that of artemisias.

DILL

Known as: Dill *(Anethum graveolens)*
Plant type: Annual

Dill is worth growing just for its feathery foliage, so its airy heads of chartreuse blooms are an added bonus. Of course, its fresh fragrance is a welcome addition to the garden, too!

Dill

What it looks like. Dill plants produce hollow stems bearing finely cut green leaves. In summer, the stems are topped with many-branched clusters of tiny yellow-green flowers. All parts of the plant are aromatic.

Which one to choose. 'Bouquet' is a popular cultivar with blue-tinged green leaves and large flower heads on 3- to 4-foot stems. 'Fernleaf' is a better choice if you're more interested in foliage. Growing to only 18 inches tall, this compact cultivar is much slower to produce blooms, so it looks good over a longer period.

Where to plant it. Dill performs well in both full sun and light shade. Average, well-drained soil is fine.

How to grow it. Dill doesn't appreciate transplanting, so you'll get the best results by sowing the seed directly in your garden. In most areas, plant outdoors in early spring to midsummer; fall to late-winter planting works best south of Zone 8. Scatter the seed evenly over the planting area, press it into the soil, and keep it evenly moist until sprouts appear. Don't worry about thinning the seedlings; a bit of crowding will allow the plants to support each other.

How to use it. This easy annual herb works well as a filler for the middle or back of a flower bed or border. It's especially handy for planting around young perennials and shrubs, so you get the temporary foliage and floral interest until the longer-lasting plants fill in. Dill is popular with some butterflies (it provides food for their caterpillers). Another real plus with this herb is that dill is said to be deer resistant.

What to plant with it. Dill's airy yellowish flower clusters look great paired with large, showy blooms, such as anise hyssop, roses, or purple coneflowers. Enjoy the finely cut foliage as a pleasing contrast to herbs with broad leaves, such as those of nasturtiums, sages, and sorrels. Try it with the dark purple leaves of 'Purple Ruffles' basil for a particularly striking partnership.

A Real Volunteer

Dill readily self-sows, so deadhead individual clusters or pull out whole plants when the flowers begin to fade.

FENNEL

Fennel

Known as: Fennel, common fennel
(Foeniculum vulgare)

Plant type: Perennial

I like to think of fennel as dill with an attitude: It has a similar airy appearance, but it's bigger, bushier, and longer lasting than its annual cousin.

What it looks like. Fennel forms tight clumps of upright stems growing 4 to 6 feet tall, with finely cut foliage that has a definite licorice scent. Tiny yellow flowers held in many-branched, flat-topped clusters bloom in mid- to late summer.

Which one to choose. Common fennel's foliage is a bright, fresh-looking green that's quite attractive in its own right. But if you're looking for something really striking, I highly recommend bronze fennel (*Foeniculum vulgare* 'Purpureum'). It's identical to the regular green form, except that the stems and leaves are a wonderful reddish brown color. Both are usually hardy in Zones 5 to 9.

Where to plant it. Give fennel a site with average, well-drained soil and full sun. It will also grow in light shade, but the stems may be weaker and more prone to wind damage.

How to grow it. While fennel is perennial in a wide range of climates, it grows so quickly that you can use it as an annual just about anywhere. It grows from deep taproots that don't like transplanting, so it's best to sow the seed directly in the garden in mid- to late spring. Cover with soil and keep moist until seedlings appear.

Regular deadheading is critical to keep fennel from self-sowing and becoming weedy. If you forget to deadhead and are faced with a small forest of fennel seedlings, be sure to remove them when they're young; they're hard to pull out once established.

How to use it. Fennel's feathery foliage and upright form makes it a handsome background plant for a flower border. Enjoy the compact, leafy growth of 'Fernleaf' in the middle of the border or in a container. Fennel is a favorite food plant for the larvae of swallowtail butterflies, so it's a good addition to butterfly gardens.

What to plant with it. Pair fennel's lacy green leaves with bold flowers and foliage for an interesting contrast. Angelicas, daylilies (*Hemerocallis* species), lady's mantle, mulleins, and purple coneflowers are just a few good companions. With bronze fennel, great combinations are practically limitless: Try it with orange calendulas, bright red 'Jacob Cline' bee balm, or bright yellow 'Coronation Gold' yarrow (*Achillea* 'Coronation Gold') for an eye-catching partnership. Bronze fennel's rich brown foliage also looks amazing against chartreuse leaves, such as those of golden barberry (*Berberis thunbergii* 'Aurea').

FEVERFEW

Known as: Feverfew *(Tanacetum parthenium)*

Plant type: Perennial

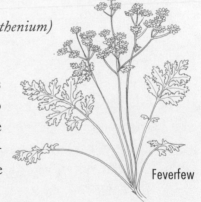
Feverfew

Feverfew's masses of tiny daisies make a cheerful contribution to sunny gardens everywhere. Where it's happy, it will self-sow enthusiastically, so you'll need to keep an eye on your feverfew plants!

What it looks like. This dependable perennial grows in clumps of sturdy, upright stems with deeply cut, aromatic leaves that resemble those of chamomile. Clusters of yellow-centered white daisies bloom from midsummer to fall.

Which one to choose. Common feverfew has bright green leaves and usually grows 2 to 3 feet tall. 'Plenum' has ruffled, white double blooms on 2-foot plants. 'Golden Ball' grows to only 1 foot tall, with dense, ball-shaped yellow blooms. 'Snowball' is similar but creamy white. My favorite, however, is golden feverfew (*Tanacetum parthenium* 'Aureum'). With its ferny, bright yellow-green foliage and single white daisies through much of the season, it's definitely on my list of top-five favorite plants. Golden feverfew tends to be more compact than other selections, growing anywhere from 8 to 18 inches tall.

Feverfew seems to be hardy in Zones 4 to 8, but it may be short-lived, lasting only two to three years. Fortunately, feverfew plants grow quickly and usually bloom the first year, so you can treat them as annuals if you wish, or let them self-sow.

Where to plant it. Feverfew grows just fine in average to poor, well-drained soil. Full sun is best, but feverfew seems to grow well in partial shade, too.

How to grow it. Deadheading is a must if you don't want a garden full of feverfew. Seedlings will pop up in the most surprising places — even in cracks in walls and paved areas. But picking off individual blooms can be a time-consuming task, so the best approach is to cut whole stems close to ground level as the blooms begin to fade. (Just leave one or two stems toward the end of the season to get a few seedlings, in case the parent plants die out.) Cutting out all the flowering stems will also encourage the growth of fresh new foliage — that's particularly a plus with golden feverfew.

Feverfew is easy to start from seed, and the cultivars will come at least partly true to the parent plant. (Golden feverfew seedlings, for instance, always have yellow-green foliage, while 'Plenum' seedlings are usually but not always double.) Sow indoors or out in early spring; do not cover the seed. Look for seedlings in one to three weeks at 70°F. Space plants about 1 foot apart.

How to use it. Feverfews make good fillers for borders and cottage gardens. The compact cultivars also make excellent edging plants. Try them in container gardens, too.

What to plant with it. The dainty daisies of this long-flowering perennial contrast well with spiky blooms, such as those of agastaches and hyssop. Golden feverfew's bright foliage makes a great base for many exciting combinations. Try it in front of purple or reddish foliage, such as purple sage. It also looks smashing with bright purple or blue blooms, such as Carpathian bellflowers *(Campanula carpatica)* or Johnny-jump-ups *(Viola tricolor)*.

GERANIUMS, SCENTED

Known as: Rose geranium *(Pelargonium graveolens)*, lemon geranium *(P. crispum)*, citronella geranium *(P. citronellum)*, lime geranium *(P. nervosum)*, peppermint geranium *(P. tomentosum)*, nutmeg geranium *(P. fragrans)*, apple geranium *(P. odoratissimum)*, coconut geranium *(P. grossularioides)*

Rose geranium

Plant type: Annual

If I could grow only one genus of fragrant plants, it would be scented geraniums. This diverse group offers an incredible variety of heights, habits, colors, and aromas.

What they look like. It's difficult to give a general description of scented geraniums, since they all look so different. By definition, though, they all have fragrant leaves that release their scent when rubbed. Another trait scented geraniums share is their intolerance of frost. Fortunately, they make great container plants, so it's easy to overwinter them indoors.

Which ones to choose. With hundreds of species and cultivars to choose from, where do you start? I've described a few of my favorites below, but I've never found a scented geranium I didn't like!

I recommend beginning a collection by buying any that you can get your hands on locally. It's really best to purchase the plants in person, so you can rub the leaves before you buy and pick the fragrances you find most appealing. After that, check the catalogs of mail-order herb nurseries to find some of the more unusual selections.

Of all the scented geraniums, rose geranium *(Pelargonium graveolens)* is probably the most widely available. Its deeply cut green leaves have a strong rose aroma, and the pink flowers are pretty, too. This plant grows vigorously and forms large clumps — up to 3 feet tall and wide in a large container. 'Grey Lady Plymouth' is similar but has a creamy white edging on the leaves. 'Atomic Snowflake' (sometimes sold just as 'Snowflake') has rounded, bright green leaves with white streaks and a lemony rose scent. 'Rober's Lemon Rose' has a similar fragrance but irregularly lobed green leaves.

Another widely available species is lemon geranium *(P. crispum),* with lavender blooms and powerfully lemon-scented leaves tightly packed on strongly upright stems to 3 feet tall. Citronella geranium *(P. citronellum)* has purple-pink flowers and large, deeply cut, strongly lemon-scented foliage that repels mosquitoes. Lime geranium *(P. nervosum)* produces bushy, rounded plants with lavender flowers and small, toothed green leaves that have a lemon-lime scent.

One of my particular favorites is peppermint geranium *(P. tomentosum),* with small white flowers and broad, velvety foliage that has a strong peppermint scent. Unlike most scented geraniums, this one seems to prefer — instead of just tolerate — partial shade. It also has a trailing habit that looks great spilling out of a container or window box. 'Chocolate Mint' has dark purple blotches in the leaves.

Another particularly wonderful species is nutmeg geranium *(P. fragrans).* It has a bushy, trailing habit, long-lasting white blooms, and small, gray-green leaves with a warm, spicy scent. 'Variegatum' has cream-streaked foliage. Apple geranium *(P. odoratissimum)* has a similar habit and flowers, but the olive-green leaves have a pronounced fruity scent. Coconut geranium *(P. grossularioides)* is another compact, delicate-looking species, with tiny lavender-pink flowers and dark green, crinkled, aromatic leaves.

Where to plant them. As a group, scented geraniums prefer full sun and average, well-drained soil. A steady supply of moisture will encourage vigorous growth, but avoid sites with soggy soil.

How to grow them. Scented geraniums benefit from occasional pinching and deadheading to encourage bushier growth. Make sure you bring them indoors before frost if you want to keep them from year to year. Keeping them in pots year-round makes moving them in and out relatively easy. If you prefer to plant them out in the garden, do so after the last spring frost, then dig them up and pot them again in late summer to early fall, or take cuttings in summer and overwinter those small plants indoors. Indoors, keep scented geraniums on a bright windowsill or under lights and provide good air circulation. Container-grown geraniums benefit from monthly feedings of an organic liquid fertilizer, applied according to the label directions.

Seed-grown geraniums often vary in scent, so the best way to reproduce your favorite fragrances is to take cuttings in spring or summer. Mature plants sometimes send up suckers near their base, and you can carefully remove these (make sure you get some roots) and transplant them.

How to use them. Plant scented geraniums near the front of a bed or border, along a path, near a doorway, or in containers on a deck or patio. The upright forms, such as lemon geranium, look great trained into potted standards (miniature single-stemmed "trees" with bushy tops). Try the bushy, trailing types, including peppermint, nutmeg, apple, and coconut, in window boxes or hanging baskets.

What to plant with them. The possible combinations are endless! Most scented geraniums have green leaves, so they blend well with bright flowers and colored or variegated foliage. Or consider creating groupings around a theme, such as a lemon garden, with lemon geranium, lemon basil, and yellow-leaved or variegated lemon balm (*Melissa officinalis* 'Variegatum').

Try a Topiary

To create an herb "tree," start with a young plant with a single straight stem. Insert a slender stake next to the stem, and trim the stake at the height you want the finished "head" to be. Fasten the stem to the stake with ties of yarn. Add more ties every few inches as the main shoot grows, and pinch off any side shoots that form. When the main stem reaches the desired height, pinch off the tip to encourage branching. Also pinch the tips of the resulting sideshoots every few weeks to shape the "head" of the tree. Remove the leaves along the base of the main stem for a clean trunk.

GERMANDER

Known as: Germander, common germander, wall germander *(Teucrium chamaedrys)*

Plant type: Perennial

Germander

Germander is a pretty flowering plant in its own right, but most gardeners prize it for its dense clumps of handsome evergreen foliage.

What it looks like. This Mint Family member shares its cousins' square stems and aromatic, opposite leaves. But unlike many mints, germander offers evergreen foliage. Left unpruned, plants will form a spreading mound up to 2 feet tall and wide, with pink to reddish purple flowers that bloom among the leaves toward the tips of the stems from midsummer into fall. Germander responds so well to trimming, however, that gardeners often clip it into low hedges, removing the flower buds in the process.

Which one to choose. Common germander *(Teucrium chamaedrys)* has small, oval- to wedge-shaped, glossy dark green leaves. 'Variegatum' is a striking selection with irregular yellow to creamy white splotches on the dark foliage. Prostrate germander (*T. chamaedrys* 'Prostratum') is a vigorous creeping form that grows only 6 to 10 inches tall. All of these plants are usually hardy in Zones 5 to 9.

Where to plant it. Give germander a site with full sun and average, well-drained soil. A bit of shelter will help prevent winter browning due to wind damage.

How to grow it. If you choose to shape your germander into a low hedge, start by setting out plants about 8 inches apart and pinching off the stem tips at planting time. Keep trimming every few weeks to develop and maintain the desired shape. Stop pruning in late summer, or your plants may produce tender new growth that will be prone to winter damage. (If your plants still show damage due to drying winter winds, protect them with evergreen boughs in future winters.) Prune out dead or damaged growth in spring.

Germander is slow to grow from seed, but cuttings root quickly in early to midsummer. Layering is another easy approach to starting new plants if you need only a few.

How to use it. Trimmed regularly to create a low, dense hedge, germander is a classic edging plant for flower gardens; it also looks great flanking a path. The variegated form looks good in containers, too. Creeping germander is a dainty ground cover for a sunny site.

What to plant with it. Germander's dark green foliage perfectly complements all colors of flowers. It also makes a great contrast to silver foliage, such as 'Berggarten' sage, as well as light green or yellow leaves, such as 'All Gold' lemon balm.

Variety Is the Spice of Life

If you're growing variegated germander, be sure to pinch out any all-green shoots that appear, or they'll quickly overtake the less-vigorous variegated shoots.

Hyssop

Known as: Hyssop *(Hyssopus officinalis)*
Plant type: Perennial

Hyssop's shrubby habit, fragrant foliage, and long flowering season make it a welcome addition to the herbal landscape.

What it looks like. This perennial herb grows in bushy clumps of many-branched, semi-woody stems clad in narrow, semi-evergreen to evergreen leaves that

Hyssop

have a minty but medicinal scent. You can also tell its relationship to mints by its square stems and opposite leaves. From early summer to early fall, small tubular flowers bloom in whorls in narrow spikes at the stem tips. Hyssop clumps usually grow 18 to 36 inches tall.

Which one to choose. Hyssop commonly has purple-blue blooms, but some varieties flower in pink *(Hyssopus officinalis* var. *rosea)* or white *(H. officinalis* var. *alba).* All three are generally hardy in Zones 5 to 9.

Where to plant it. Hyssop thrives in full sun but can take light shade, too. Average to dry, well-drained soil is fine.

How to grow it. Cut plants back to about 6 inches in midspring to promote bushy new growth. Trim plants again after bloom to shape them and to remove the spent flower heads. Mature plants sometimes die out suddenly, so you may want to leave a few flower heads to get self-sown seedlings for replacements.

In early spring, sow seed indoors or outdoors, ¼ inch deep. Look for seedlings in two to four weeks at 70°F. Around the last frost date, thin seedlings or set transplants to stand 12 to 18 inches apart. You can also propagate hyssop by dividing the clumps in spring or fall or by taking cuttings in early summer.

How to use it. Hyssop's handsome bushy habit and flower spikes make an excellent addition to the middle of a flower garden. It is also easy to shape hyssop into compact, aromatic hedges for edging beds, borders, and walkways. Hyssop looks great in containers, too.

What to plant with it. Contrast hyssop's dark green foliage with silver-, blue-, or yellow-leaved herbs; catmints and culinary sages are just two great companions. Bold, bright flowers, such as nasturtiums and roses, also make pretty partners for hyssop.

LADY'S MANTLES

Known as: Lady's mantle
(*Alchemilla mollis* and *A. vulgaris*)

Plant type: Perennial

Lady's mantle

These lovely perennial herbs are worth growing just for their beautiful, pleated, gray-green leaves. The airy sprays of bright yellow-green flowers are an added bonus.

What they look like. Lady's mantles produce clumps of large, fuzzy, gray-green foliage. The broad, lobed leaves are gathered where they join the stem, producing a pleated effect that's particularly noticeable on young leaves. The tiny, petalless, chartreuse flowers bloom in loose clusters in summer.

Which one to choose. The most commonly available lady's mantle is likely *Alchemilla mollis*. Its velvety foliage clumps grow anywhere from 6 to 18 inches tall, depending on the site. *A. vulgaris* (also sold as *A. xanthochlora*) is said to be slightly larger, with less-fuzzy leaves and smaller flowers, but I can't tell the two species apart! 'Auslese', a selection of *A. mollis*, has a tight, compact habit, growing to only 1 foot tall. All of these are hardy in Zones 4 to 8.

Where to plant them. Lady's mantles grow fine in partial shade, but they also perform well in full sun north of Zone 7. They appreciate evenly moist soil (especially in sun) but can tolerate dry conditions.

How to grow them. These easy-care herbs don't demand much fussing; just cut off the flower heads when they begin to die back to prevent self-sowing, or let them turn brown if you want the seedlings. It's easy to dig up these "volunteers" with a trowel; transplant them to new spots in the garden or plant them in pots to share with friends.

To grow lady's mantles from seed, sow indoors or out in early spring, covering with soil or seed-starting mix. Look for seedlings in three to four weeks at 70°F. Allow 12 to 18 inches between plants. Divide clumps in early spring in the north; fall division is fine south of Zone 6.

How to use them. Lady's mantles make great edging plants and small-scale ground covers. They also look nice in containers; just make sure to water them regularly.

What to plant with them. It's hard to think of a companion that wouldn't look good with these beautiful herbs. One of my favorite partners for lady's mantles is purple-blue flowers, such as catmints, and purple foliage, such as that of purple sage. If subtle isn't your style, try lady's mantles with bright orange calendulas or orange tulips.

A Second Chance

If lady's mantle foliage turns brown or looks tired, shear it back in midsummer to about 2 inches above the ground. New foliage will emerge within a week or two.

LAVENDERS

Known as: English lavender *(Lavandula angustifolia)*, French lavender *(L. dentata)*, Spanish lavender *(L. stoechas)*

Plant type: Perennial

Lavender

Sweetly pungent, distinctive fragrance, beautiful flowers, and handsome foliage: What more could you ask for in an herb? This old-fashioned favorite deserves a place in every herbal landscape.

What they look like. Lavenders' square stems and opposite, aromatic leaves show their relationship to other Mint Family members. The woody, base-branching stems bear narrow leaves and are topped with spikes of tiny tubular flowers.

Which one to choose. Lavender lovers have dozens of species and cultivars to choose from. English lavender *(Lavandula angustifolia)* is perhaps the most common, growing 1 to 3 feet tall with silver-green foliage and purple flowers from early to mid- or late summer. Deep purple 'Hidcote' and lighter purple-blue 'Munstead' are compact cultivars, growing 12 to 15 inches tall. (These cultivars are usually raised from seed, so they can vary somewhat in height, habit, and color.) 'Lady' is a seed strain that grows quickly and blooms the first year, with purple-blue flowers over grayish green leaves on 10- to 12-inch plants. It's a great choice if you tend to have trouble overwintering lavenders outdoors, because you can start new plants each year and still have flowers by midsummer. 'Jean Davis' grows 18 inches tall and has pinkish white flowers. All of these are generally hardy in Zones 5 to 9.

'Provence' *(L. × intermedia)* is a hybrid between *L. angustifolia* and *L. latifolia.* Hardy in Zones 5 to 8, it grows 2 to 3 feet tall, with purple-blue blooms and intensely aromatic, silver-gray foliage.

French lavender *(L. dentata)* is much more tender, usually hardy only south of Zone 7. It's definitely worth growing even as an annual, for its light purple flowers and narrow, gray-green leaves with fringed edges. Clumps grow quickly to 3 feet tall. 'Candicans' is a selection with very silvery leaves. 'Linda Ligon' is a beautiful French lavender with creamy yellow splashes on the leaves.

Spanish lavender *(L. stoechas)* is another handsome, tender species, with aromatic, very narrow gray leaves and dark violet flowers on plants to about 18 inches tall. This species is hardy south of Zone 7. My favorite lavender, *L. stoechas* var. *pedunculata*, has dense flower heads topped with inch-long purple "ears." In full bloom, the plants look like silvery shrubs topped with a herd of purple bunny heads!

Where to plant them. Lavenders grow best in a dry and well-drained, sunny location. They will not tolerate soggy soil, so they can be difficult to grow in rainy climates, especially where winters tend to be wet instead of snowy. And while they thrive in dry heat, they suffer in the humid summers of the south.

How to grow them. Deadheading after the first flush of flowers can encourage rebloom on some lavenders. Snip off individual flower stems or gather several stems in your hand and cut them off with pruning shears. Trimming over the whole plant with hedge shears is another option. Avoid trimming after late summer, or your plants may produce tender new growth that is prone to winter damage. Wait until new growth is emerging in mid- to late spring before pruning to remove remaining seed heads and to shape the clumps.

Mulching lavenders with an inch or two of sand or gravel can help keep the base of the plants dry and discourage rot.

The fastest way to reproduce lavenders is by taking cuttings in summer. Layering is another good approach, but it takes longer and gives only a few new plants. If you need lots of plants and don't mind some variability, you can grow lavenders from seed. Sow outdoors in early fall or early spring, just covering with soil. Or sow indoors in late winter; then enclose the pots in a plastic bag and refrigerate them for a month or two. Place the pots in a bright place at 60°F; look for seedlings in two to four weeks. Space compact lavenders 12 inches apart; leave 18 inches between larger plants.

How to use them. Hardy lavenders are beautiful additions to the front or middle of a bed or border. Try the compact cultivars for edging walks or flower gardens; you can even trim them into small hedges. Lavenders also make great container plants. French and Spanish lavender are particularly nice as houseplants in winter; just keep the soil on the dry side.

What to plant with them. These beloved herbs pair perfectly with a wide range of beautiful companions, including hardy geraniums (*Geranium* species), pinks (*Dianthus* species), lamb's ears *(Stachys byzantina),* and thymes, just to name a few. Roses and lavender are a classic cottage-garden combination.

LEMON BALM

Known as: Lemon balm *(Melissa officinalis)*

Plant type: Perennial

Lemon balm

Lemon balm's bright green leaves and tiny flowers aren't especially ornamental, but you'll enjoy this easy-to-grow herb for its powerful lemon fragrance. It's a joy planted along a path, where you'll release the scent as you brush by it.

What it looks like. This vigorous perennial will readily spread throughout a border. Like other Mint Family members, lemon balm has square stems and aromatic, opposite leaves. The glossy, oval, almost heart-shaped leaves have slightly toothed edges. The mid- to late-summer flowers are small and white — not very showy. Plants generally grow 2 to 3 feet tall and about 2 feet wide.

Which one to choose. Common lemon balm *(Melissa officinalis)* produces plain green leaves. 'Variegata' (also sold as 'Aurea') is more interesting, with yellow frosting on the edges of green leaves. But my favorite is definitely the cultivar 'All Gold', with bright yellow foliage. All are generally hardy in Zones 5 to 9.

Where to plant it. Lemon balm grows in partial shade to full sun. It thrives in evenly moist soil but also tolerates average to dry soil.

How to grow it. Deadheading is a must to keep your lemon balm from seeding everywhere. As soon as you see the flowers forming, cut all of the stems back to about 2 inches above the ground; the plants will quickly produce new foliage.

Powdery mildew can be a problem, causing dusty gray patches on leaves. Cut back affected plants to a few inches above the ground to get a flush of clean new foliage.

Lemon balm roots easily from cuttings in early summer. You can also divide clumps in early spring. To grow plants from seed, sow outdoors in fall or indoors in late winter; do not cover. Outdoors, look for seedlings the following spring; indoors, expect germination in two to three weeks at 70°F. Allow 12 to 18 inches between plants.

How to use it. Common lemon balm isn't particularly showy, but it can be a soothing green addition to a cottage garden or other colorful planting. 'Variegata' and 'All Gold' look great in containers; just make sure you keep them watered!

What to plant with it. Pair common lemon balm with colorful flowers or variegated foliage, such as pineapple mint. Combine 'Variegata' or 'All Gold' with purple-blue flowers, such as ajugas (*Ajuga* species) and bellflowers (*Campanula* species), or purple foliage, such as 'Purple Ruffles' basil.

MINTS

Peppermint

Known as: Peppermint *(Mentha × piperita)*, spearmint *(M. spicata)*, Corsican mint *(M. requienii)*, pennyroyal *(M. pulegium)*, pineapple mint (*M. suaveolens* 'Variegata'), ginger mint (*M. × gentilis* 'Variegata')

Plant type: Perennial

It's hard to imagine a fragrance garden without at least one mint! Yes, these vigorous spreaders can be a problem if left unsupervised, but in the right spot, they're a must-have if you enjoy scented herbs.

What they look like. Mints and their relatives share several distinctive features, including square stems and opposite, aromatic leaves. They also produce dense spikes of tiny flowers in whorls at the leaf joints along the upper parts of the stems. Other than that, mints vary widely in leaf shapes and colors, heights, and habits.

Which one to choose. There are hundreds of different mints to choose from, but be careful — different nurseries often sell the same plant under different names. It's best to buy mints where you can see and sniff them to choose your favorites.

If fragrance is your main interest, peppermint *(Mentha × piperita)* is a good place to start. It has dark green leaves often flushed with red and spikes of lilac-pink flowers on 2-foot stems. 'Blackstem' has very dark leaves and nearly black stems. 'Variegata' has creamy splashes on the leaves. Spearmint *(M. spicata)*, a parent of peppermint, has bright green, wrinkled leaves and spikes of pinkish to purplish flowers on 1- to 3-foot stems. The leaves of 'Crispa' are particularly crinkled. You'll find many other flavor selections of these herb-garden staples, including 'Chocolate Mint' (some claim it has a dark-chocolate undertone), 'Double Mint' (a blend of peppermint and spearmint flavors), and 'Lavender Mint' (with a lavender-peppermint scent). All of these are generally hardy in Zones 5 to 9.

Spearmint

Perhaps the most powerfully mint-scented species is Corsican mint *(M. requienii).* At first glance, you might not even guess it's a mint: This tiny perennial forms carpets of rounded leaves and tiny lilac flowers on spreading stems to barely 1 inch tall. This species is hardy in Zones 7 to 9.

Pennyroyal *(M. pulegium)* is another carpet-forming mint, but it's not nearly as low as Corsican mint. Pennyroyal starts as dense mats of glossy green leaves on long, trailing shoots. In summer, these creepers produce more-upright shoots usually 6 to 10 inches tall. Lilac-pink flowers bloom in whorls along these stems. Pennyroyal is usually hardy in Zones 5 to 9.

Two kinds of mint that have particularly ornamental foliage include pineapple mint (*M. suaveolens* 'Variegata') and variegated ginger mint (*M. × gentilis* 'Variegata'). Pineapple mint doesn't have much flavor, but it does have a sweet pineapple aroma. Its woolly, bright green leaves are irregularly edged in cream or white. Variegated ginger mint's oval, dark green leaves are splashed with yellow, particularly along the

Pennyroyal

leaf veins. Both of these mints form showy, spreading clumps about 18 inches tall and usually are hardy in Zones 5 to 9.

Where to plant them. These adaptable herbs can grow practically anywhere, from full sun to shade, but most mints prefer partial shade and evenly moist soil. Pineapple mint seems to tolerate drier soil than most other mints.

How to grow them. The most important thing to know about mints is that they spread, and spread fast! If possible, give your mints a spot where they can spread freely. If that isn't an option, plant them within a root barrier (such as a bottomless bucket sunk in the soil almost to the rim) to help control the spread of the creeping stems. Eventually, the stems will sneak over or under most barriers, so keep an eye on them and pull or cut out unwanted stems. Dividing clumps every year or two can also help control their spread.

If the foliage begins to look dull or discolored, cut back the stems by one-half to two-thirds in midsummer. This summer shearing will encourage a flush of fresh growth.

In the northern parts of their hardiness ranges, most mints benefit from a lightweight winter mulch, such as evergreen branches.

How to use them. Enjoy mints as space-fillers in cottage gardens or semi-wild areas. Try planting them along a stepping-stone path, letting them creep between the stones, and mow regularly to keep the path clear. When you walk along the path, you'll enjoy the aroma released as you step on or brush by the plants. Corsican mint's ground-hugging habit makes it especially nice for planting along paths, since it won't need trimming. Pennyroyal makes an attractive low-growing ground cover, particularly where you want a rampant spreader; it also looks great in a hanging basket.

What to plant with them. Because they spread quickly, mints can overpower less-vigorous companions unless you control their creeping stems with some kind of barrier. Try them with sturdy companions, such as hostas, or with other spreaders, such as bee balms.

MULLEINS

Known as: Common mullein, flannel plant, velvet plant, Aaron's rod, hag tape, torches (*Verbascum* species)

Plant type: Biennial

Mullein

With their handsome foliage rosettes and tall, showy flower spikes, mulleins make an eye-catching addition to an herbal landscape.

What they look like. These biennial or perennial herbs start out as 2-foot-wide rosettes of long, broad, semi-evergreen or evergreen leaves. The foliage may be green and relatively smooth or covered with silvery gray hairs. After the first year, 3- to 6-foot flower spikes rise from the center of each clump, blooming from early to late summer.

Which one to choose. Among the fuzzy-leaved mulleins, *Verbascum thapsus* is one of the most commonly seen species. It has hairy, gray-green leaves and 6-foot stems with bright yellow flowers that open at irregular intervals along a dense spike. This biennial species self-sows prolifically and can quickly become weedy if not deadheaded. Biennial *V. bombyciferum* and short-lived perennial Olympic mullein (*V. olympicum*) has very silvery foliage and bright yellow blooms on 4- to 6-foot spikes. These are all generally hardy in Zones 5 to 9.

Smoother-leaved mulleins are also great garden plants. *V. chaixii* grows to about 3 feet tall, with gray-green foliage and branching spikes of light yellow blooms with fuzzy purple centers. 'Album' has purple-centered white flowers. *V. phoeniceum* bears green leaves and spikes of purple blooms on 3-foot spikes. 'Flush of White' produces pure white blooms on 24- to 30-inch stems. It will bloom the first year if you start the seed indoors in early spring. My all-time favorite green-leaved mullein is 'Southern Charm'. These 2- to 3-foot hybrids bloom in a range of sunset colors, from soft yellow and peach through rosy pink and lavender. All of these short-lived perennials are usually hardy in Zones 5 to 9.

Where to plant them. Mulleins will grow in almost any soil that isn't soggy; good drainage is important. They tolerate light shade, but full sun produces the best growth and flowering. If possible, site mulleins in a sheltered spot; otherwise, wind might topple over the tall flower spikes.

How to grow them. Removing faded flower spikes will prevent self-sowing and can encourage rebloom. Just leave one spike to set seed so you'll have a few seedlings to replace the parent plant when it dies. Pull out any unwanted seedlings while they are still small.

Sow mullein seed outdoors or indoors in early spring, barely covering it with a sprinkling of soil or seed-starting mix. Look for seedlings in two to four weeks at 60°F. Thin seedlings or space transplants to stand about 18 inches apart. Move mullein seedlings while they are young; older plants have deep roots that are prone to damage during transplanting.

How to use them. Mulleins look great in masses, sited at the back of a border, or planted alone as a landscape accent.

What to plant with them. Contrast mulleins' bold form and broad foliage with more delicate perennials, such as purple-blue catmints. Tall cosmos *(Cosmos bipinnatus)* in white and shades of pink also make pretty partners at the back of the border. For a charming silver-and-gold composition, combine silver-leaved mullein with 'Powis Castle' artemisia and 'Coronation Gold' yarrow.

NASTURTIUM

Known as: Garden nasturtium
(Tropaeolum majus)
Plant type: Annual

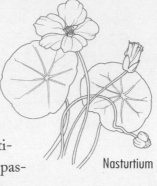
Nasturtium

These easy-to-grow annuals are worth growing just for their distintive round leaves, but they also produce beautiful flowers in a range of jewel tones and pastel color combinations.

What it looks like. Nasturtiums produce circular green leaves, each joined at the center to a separate stem, like a bunch of elfin umbrellas. The large blooms are funnel shaped at the base, flaring out to wide, flattened faces, usually in shades of yellow, orange, or red. The single, semi-double, or double flowers, which often have a sweet scent, start blooming in early to midsummer and continue until frost. Some plants form bushy, 8- to 12-inch-tall clumps; others have trailing stems that reach to 6 feet or more.

Which one to choose. There are many wonderful cultivars to choose from, in a wide range of sizes and colors. 'Whirlybird Mixed' is a popular 1-foot-tall strain with large, upright-facing, single flowers held well above the bushy foliage. 'Jewel Mixed' is similar but slightly more compact, growing to about 9 inches tall. 'Alaska' has semi-double blooms in mixed colors among cream-marbled leaves on bushy, 1-foot plants. 'Double Gleam Hybrids Mixed' offers fragrant, double yellow, orange, or red flowers on semi-trailing stems to about 15 inches long.

If you're looking for a specific color, rather than mixes, you can find those, too. 'Empress of India' is a classic cultivar with crimson flowers and dark blue-green foliage. Some sources describe this as having trailing stems, but the seeds I've purchased under this name have always grown into bushy, 1-foot plants. 'Peach Melba' is also very pretty, with 1-foot plants that produce creamy yellow single flowers with raspberry-streaked throats. My favorite nasturtium is

'Tip Top Mahogany', which has deep red blooms and chartreuse leaves in bushy 1-foot clumps.

Where to plant it. Nasturtiums bloom best in full sun and average to dry, well-drained soil. They will also grow in partly shaded, moist sites, but they'll tend to produce lush clumps of foliage with few flowers. (Of course, that might be desirable if you're growing a selection with interesting foliage, such as 'Alaska'.)

How to grow it. For an extra-early start, sow seed indoors in early spring; otherwise, sow seed directly in the garden around your last frost date. Sow the seed about ½ inch deep. Thin seedlings or set transplants to stand 6 to 9 inches apart. Sometimes aphids attack nasturtiums, congregating on buds, flowers, and the undersides of leaves. Spray infested plants with insecticidal soap. (Don't spray flowers or leaves you plan to eat.) Other than that, nasturtiums need virtually no care.

How to use it. Trailing nasturtiums are super for covering difficult or unsightly areas, such as rock piles or stony slopes. They also look great weaving among other herbs and flowers in mixed plantings. Bushy nasturtiums are excellent near the front of beds and borders. Both kinds of nasturtiums grow well in window boxes, hanging baskets, and other containers. Add them to kitchen gardens, too, for their edible leaves and flowers, which have a slightly peppery taste.

What to plant with it. Combine nasturtiums with other sunny-colored flowers, such as bee balms or calendulas, or pair them with plainer herbs, such as parsley and sorrels. Their circular leaves contrast well with fine-textured foliage, such as that of dill and rosemary. Bronze fennel, purple sage, and other dark-leaved plants are particularly striking companions.

Growing Up

Trailing nasturtiums (often called climbing nasturtiums) have long stems that can also scramble their way up short arbors and trellises. I find that they appreciate netting or closely spaced strings attached to the support so they have something to wrap their leaf stems around.

OREGANOS

Known as: Common oregano *(Origanum vulgare)*, Greek oregano *(O. heracleoticum* or *O. vulgare* var. *hirtum)*, sweet marjoram *(O. majorana)*.

Plant type: Perennial

Oreganos and their relatives have long been loved for their culinary value, but many of these aromatic plants are pretty enough to earn a place in the flower garden as well.

What they look like. As a group, these perennial mint-family members share square stems and opposite, aromatic leaves. Oreganos tend to produce woody or semi-woody stems in spreading clumps. Depending upon the species, tiny purple, pink, or white flowers bloom in clusters around the stem near or at the top of the stems from midsummer to early fall.

Which one to choose. Classic herb garden oreganos include common oregano *(Origanum vulgare)*, Greek oregano (usually listed as either *O. heracleoticum* or *O. vulgare* var. *hirtum)*, and sweet marjoram *(O. majorana)*. Common oregano produces sprawling clumps of medium green leaves that generally have a mild oregano scent. The white, pink, or purple flowers bloom in clusters in summer atop 18- to 24-inch stems. This perennial is hardy in Zones 5 to 9. Greek oregano is a perennial with small, pungent, dark green leaves and small, white summer flowers on 1- to 2-foot stems. It is generally hardy in Zones 5 to 9. Sweet marjoram is a tender perennial (hardy south of Zone 8) with oval, gray-green, aromatic foliage and clusters of white or pinkish summer flowers on 1- to 2-foot stems.

All of the above herbs are pretty in a subtle way, but if you're looking for more impact, consider some of the ornamental oreganos. 'Hopleys' or 'Hopleys Purple', often listed as a cultivar of *O. laevigatum*, grows 1 to 2 feet tall with loose clumps of reddish stems clad in dark green leaves. Blooming later than most oreganos, usually late summer through fall, the purplish pink flowers are surrounded by

Oregano

long-lasting, purple-red bracts. 'Herrenhausen' is a popular 1- to 2-foot hybrid with bright reddish pink flowers and purple-red bracts from late summer through fall. Cool weather often brings out a purple or reddish blush on the aromatic leaves of these two cultivars. Figure on Zones 5 to 9 for hardiness.

My favorite oreganos are the yellow-leaved selections. The one commonly called golden oregano (*O. vulgare* 'Aureum') is yellow-green in partial shade and quite yellow in full sun, with pinkish flowers. 'Norton's Gold' is a wonderful hybrid that stays bright gold even in partial shade, especially on the new growth. Both of these cultivars tend to grow only 8 to 12 inches tall, and they appreciate some midday shade in hot-summer climates. Both should be hardy in Zones 5 to 9.

Where to plant them. Oreganos and their relatives grow best in full sun and average to dry, well-drained soil. Most will also take light shade, but the stems will tend to flop. Good drainage is especially important in winter.

How to grow them. In spring, cut out the dead wood and trim the remaining flower stalks down to about 1 inch above the ground. Pinching the shoot tips in late spring to early summer will promote bushier growth. Divide clumps every three to four years in spring to keep them vigorous.

The best way to propagate perennial oreganos is to divide their clumps in spring or take cuttings in early summer. Space plants about 1 foot apart. Start marjoram seed indoors in midspring, just covering it; look for seedlings in about a week at 70°F. Two or three weeks after the last frost date, set seedlings out in clumps spaced 6 to 8 inches apart.

How to use them. Plant oreganos along a path or at the front of the border where you can brush the leaves and enjoy their aroma. Their flowers are ideal for attracting butterflies to your garden. Oreganos also make great container plants. Include the spicy-scented types in a kitchen garden for seasoning meats and Italian dishes.

What to plant with them. Pair the plainer culinary oreganos with bright flowers, such as marigolds (*Tagetes* species). The showier blooms of ornamental oreganos combine well with anise hyssop, purple coneflower, and yarrows. The yellow-leaved oreganos make a striking contrast to dark foliage; try interplanting them with a red-leaved lettuce, such as 'Merlot'.

PARSLEY

Known as: Curly parsley *(Petroselinum crispum* var. *crispum)* flat-leaved parsley *(P. crispum* var. *neopolitanum)*

Plant type: Biennial

Parsley doesn't rank high in the fabulous-flower department, but its dense clumps of bright green foliage are ideal for edgings or fillers in bloom-filled beds and borders.

Curly parsley

What it looks like. This biennial herb produces rosettes of aromatic, long-stalked green leaves the first year. The foliage clumps usually grow 6 to 10 inches tall and about as wide. In their second summer, 12- to 18-inch stalks rise from the center of the rosette, topped with airy clusters of tiny yellow flowers.

Which one to choose. Parsley comes in two basic forms: flat-leaved, which is also called Italian *(Petroselinum crispum* var. *neopolitanum),* and curled *(P. crispum* var. *crispum).* You're probably already familiar with curly parsley as a garnish, but its tightly crinkled leaves also look great in the garden. Flat-leaved parsley's glossy foliage is more flavorful but not quite as ornamental.

Flat-leaved parsley

Where to plant it. Parsley thrives in full sun to light shade and average to moist, well-drained soil.

How to grow it. Mulching parsley in winter and removing the second-year flower stems helps the clumps last through a second season. In my experience, though, it's easier to start with new plants each year. Plus, if you plan to eat it, it will be bitter the second year.

Sow seed outdoors in early fall or early spring or indoors in early spring. Soaking the seed in warm water overnight can speed up germination. Sow seed ¼ inch deep. Look for sprouts in three to four weeks at 70°F. Set the seedlings outdoors around the time of your last frost date, then thin the seedlings or set transplants to stand 8 to 12 inches apart.

How to use it. Plant a row of parsley to make a tidy green edging for a flower bed or border. It also looks good growing along a walkway or in a container.

What to plant with it. Create colorful foliage combinations by pairing parsley with yellow-leaved plants, such as golden oregano or golden hostas. Parsley's bright green leaves also make a cool contrast to white flowers or white-variegated foliage. Try it with white pansies or pineapple mint.

PURPLE CONEFLOWERS

Known as: Coneflower (*Echinacea* species)

Plant type: Perennial

There's nothing subtle about these showy perennial herbs! While interest in their healing properties has exploded in recent years, purple coneflowers have long been appreciated by herb and flower lovers alike.

Purple coneflower

What they look like. Purple coneflowers produce large, daisylike flowers with orange-bronze center cones surrounded by rose-pink (not purple, in spite of their name) petals. These long-lasting flowers bloom from mid- to late summer atop straight, stiff stems that rise from a thick clump of dark green leaves. Even when the petals drop, the center cones remain to add interest.

Which one to choose. The species you are most likely to find for sale is *Echinacea purpurea*. Native to the Midwestern plains of North

America, this species has broadly lance-shaped, coarsely toothed leaves and 3- to 5-foot stems topped with flowers that have slightly drooping petals. 'Magnus' is supposed to have large, strong, reddish pink flowers with extrawide petals that are held horizontally, rather than drooping. 'Robert Bloom', also with bright flowers and horizontal petals, is a vegetatively propagated selection, so it is more uniform. 'White Lustre' and 'White Swan' are white-petaled forms of purple coneflower. All of these are hardy in Zones 3 to 9.

You might run across several other species in mail-order catalogs. Narrow-leaved purple coneflower *(E. angustifolia)* is relatively compact, usually growing 12 to 18 inches tall, but is otherwise similar to *E. purpurea*. Figure on Zones 4 to 9 for hardiness. Pale coneflower *(E. pallida)* grows 3 to 4 feet tall, with narrow, pale pink drooping petals around the central cone. It should be hardy in Zones 5 to 9. And then there's *E. paradoxa*, a purple coneflower with yellow petals! Height is 3 to 4 feet; hardiness is usually Zones 6 to 9.

Where to plant them. Purple coneflowers thrive in full sun but can also tolerate light shade. Average to poor soil is fine. You'll often see purple coneflowers touted as drought resistant, but they really do best (at least for me) in evenly moist soil. Good drainage is a must, though; they hate soggy soil, especially in winter.

How to grow them. Deadheading the spent flowers for the first few weeks can help extend the bloom season. After that, consider leaving some of the seed heads to add winter interest and attract birds (especially goldfinches).

Purple coneflowers seldom need division; in fact, they seem to do better without it. If you want more plants of specific cultivars, it's best to buy them. But if you don't mind some variability, seed is another option. You'll find much contradictory information on starting these plants from seed; some say they are difficult, while others say they are as easy as marigolds! Purple coneflowers self-sow readily in my garden, so I usually follow their example and plant the seed outdoors (just covered with soil) in fall or late winter for seedlings the following spring. If you sow indoors in late winter or early spring, try placing the pots in plastic bags in your refrigerator and chilling them for four to six weeks before moving them to room temperature. Look for seedlings in three to four weeks at 65°F. Thin seedlings or set transplants to stand about 18 inches apart.

How to use them. Purple coneflowers look great in both formal and informal gardens. Besides adding welcome color, they are also popular with bees and butterflies. Just site them behind lower-growing plants to hide their not-especially-interesting foliage.

A Trick for Later, Longer Bloom Time

Cutting purple coneflowers back by half in early summer can delay their bloom season several weeks, giving a later and longer show, because the sun is usually not so intense when they bloom later.

What to plant with them. Purple coneflowers combine beautifully with ornamental grasses as well as colorful perennials, such as garden phlox *(Phlox paniculata)*, pink 'Marshall's Delight' bee balm, and yarrows. Try purple coneflowers with the feathery brown foliage of bronze fennel to echo the bronze centers and contrast with the bold form of the flowers. Enjoy the white-flowered selections in an evening garden with other white flowers and with silvery foliage, such as lamb's ears.

ROSEMARY

Known as: Rosemary *(Rosmarinus officinalis)*

Plant type: Tender perennial

If you enjoy fragrant plants, you need rosemary in your garden! Be sure to site this aromatic herb within easy reach, because you'll want to brush by it often.

What it looks like. Rosemary is an attractive evergreen shrub with woody stems and narrow, leathery, dark green leaves that have a pungent piney scent. Small flowers, usually blue, bloom along the upper parts of the stems. South of Zone 7,

Rosemary

where rosemary generally grows outdoors year-round, height is around 3 to 5 feet and bloom time is usually from late winter to early spring. If you bring rosemary indoors for the winter, expect flowers in spring and summer. Its size depends on how big a pot you give it and how much you prune it.

Which one to choose. *Rosmarinus officinalis* has yielded dozens of selections varying in hardiness, color, and habit. 'Arp' is reputed to be one of the hardiest cultivars, usually overwintering in Zone 7. 'Hill Hardy' and 'Salem' are two others to look for if hardiness is your prime consideration.

While light blue is the most common flower color, you can find selections in shades from light to dark blue, as well as pink or white. 'Tuscan Blue', for example, has particularly dark blue flowers. 'Majorca Pink' has pink flowers; 'Albus' is white. You can even find cultivars with variegated, gold-edged leaves, under the names 'Golden Rain' and 'Joyce DeBaggio'.

Most rosemaries have an upright, bushy habit, but several have a low, trailing habit. 'Prostratus' is the most common creeping rosemary. 'Lockwood de Forest' has glossy, dark green leaves and light blue flowers; 'Renzels' (Irene®) is similar, but with deeper blue flowers.

Where to plant it. Rosemary requires full sun and average soil. Excellent drainage is a must; even in warm regions, plants may survive winter cold only to succumb to rot in soggy spring soil. North of Zone 8, it's best to grow rosemary in containers and bring it indoors to a sunny windowsill for the winter.

How to grow it. Prune plants lightly as needed to shape them. Otherwise, rosemary needs little care.

It's possible to grow rosemary from seed: Sow ¼ inch deep indoors in late winter. Look for seedlings in three to four weeks at 70°F. Seedlings will vary in size and color. For faster, more consistent results, take cuttings from nonflowering stems in early summer, or layer (see page 147). In the garden, space plants 1 to 3 feet apart.

How to use it. Where rosemary is winter-hardy, enjoy it as a hedge or grow it as a small shrub. The creeping types look great as ground covers or trailing over walls. Elsewhere, use bushy rosemaries for summer interest in beds and borders, or enjoy them as container plants. Creeping rosemary looks great in window boxes and hanging baskets. If you like to cook, rosemary is a versatile must-have in the kitchen garden.

What to plant with it. Contrast this herb's narrow, dark green leaves with broad or lacy, silvery foliage, such as that of artemisias or lamb's ears. Rosemary also makes a handsome partner for more colorful flowering plants, such as nasturtiums.

RUE

Known as: Common rue, herb-of-grace
(*Ruta graveolens*)

Plant type: Perennial

Rue's beautiful blue-green leaves are hard to beat if you're looking for fabulous foliage. But this handsome herb isn't just a foliage plant — it offers yellow flowers, too!

Rue

What it looks like. Rue grows in shrubby, 3-foot-tall clumps of deeply divided, blue-green leaves that are evergreen or semi-evergreen. The foliage releases a bitter scent when you brush it, and some people experience skin irritation after touching it, so it's definitely not an herb to plant close to a path. Four-petaled, greenish yellow flowers appear in clusters in summer.

Which one to choose. While the straight species is certainly a worthwhile garden plant, specialty nurseries also offer unusual selections. 'Jackman's Blue', for instance, has particularly blue-gray leaves and tends to be more compact than the species. 'Blue Curl' has slightly curled leaves. The foliage of 'Variegata' is irregularly splashed with white, with the occasional all-white leaf or shoot. All of these are hardy in Zones 4 to 9.

Where to plant it. Rue prefers average, well-drained soil in full sun, although it will tolerate light shade.

How to grow it. In mid- to late spring, cut out dead shoots and cut the stems back by half to two-thirds to shape the plant. Make your cuts just above where new growth is emerging. Wearing long sleeves and gloves to protect your skin, prune or shear off the spent flowers to prevent self-sowing (or leave a few blooms if you want a few new plants).

If you don't get self-sown seedlings, sow rue seed indoors in early spring, just covering it. Look for seedlings in three to five weeks at 70°F. Set plants about 18 inches apart. You can also take cuttings in mid- to late summer.

How to use it. Rue's lovely foliage is an excellent addition to beds and borders. Its neat mounding habit also makes it a wonderful low hedge or edging plant.

What to plant with it. You can make all kinds of great foliage combinations with rue. Create icy-cool groupings by pairing it with artemisias and other silvery-leaved plants, and include some bellflowers or other bright blue flowers as an accent. Rue's blue-green leaves and yellow-green blooms also look super with chartreuse foliage, such as golden oregano.

SAGES

Sage

Known as: Culinary sage *(Salvia officinalis)*, pineapple sage *(S. elegans)*, clary sage *(S. sclarea)*, Mexican bush sage *(S. leucantha)*

Plant type: Varies by species

It's hard to imagine an herbal garden without some sort of sage. Whether you want bright blooms, colorful foliage, or fabulous fragrance, there's a sage for every landscape.

What they look like. Like other Mint Family members, sages have square stems and opposite, aromatic leaves. Beyond that, sages vary widely in height, habit, hardiness, fragrance, and in the colors of their foliage and flower spikes.

Which one to choose. With hundreds of species and selections to choose from, it can be hard to decide which ones to try first! Culinary sage *(Salvia officinalis)* is a good place to start. It forms shrubby ever-green or semi-evergreen clumps that grow 1 to 3 feet high and about as wide. The pebbly textured, oblong, fragrant foliage is gray-green, accented by purple-blue flowers in early to midsummer. 'Albiflora' has white flowers. 'Berggarten' is a more compact selection, with much broader, rounded, silver-gray leaves. 'Purpurascens' has reddish to purple new foliage that ages to purplish green. The foliage of 'Tricolor' is irregularly marked with green, white, purplish red, and pink; the color is especially intense on the new foliage. Golden sage ('Icterina' or 'Aurea') has yellow-and-green leaves. These three colored-foliage selections are usually hardy in Zones 6 to 9; culinary sage and 'Berggarten' tend to be hardier, to Zone 4.

Other herb-garden favorites include the sweet-scented sages (also edible). Pineapple sage *(S. elegans)* is particularly popular. Besides the fragrant, bright green leaves, it also offers tubular, bright red blooms on 4-foot stems from summer to frost. 'Freida Dixon' is a selection with salmon-pink flowers. Pineapple sage is hardy only south of Zone 7, but it's great even as an annual or potted plant in northern gardens. The flowers add a pretty touch of color and a bit of flavor to fruit or green salads.

Some sages are especially prized for their flowers. Clary sage *(S. sclarea)* is a biennial with large, hairy, toothed leaves the first year and spikes of purple-and-white flowers on 2- to 3-foot stems in early summer. Mexican bush sage *(S. leucantha)* is a particularly pretty species, with showy, foot-long spikes of white flowers that emerge from a fuzzy purple calyx. They reward the gardener with months of blooms, usually from late summer or early fall to frost. The shrubby clumps of gray-green leaves grow 4 to 5 feet tall. Mexican bush sage is hardy south of Zone 7; elsewhere, enjoy it as an annual or container plant.

Where to plant them. Sages thrive in average, well-drained soil where they receive full sun.

How to grow them. Prune sage plants back by one-half to two-thirds in midspring, making your cuts just above where new growth is emerging. Pinching out shoot tips in late spring or early summer encourages bushier growth, if desired. Other than that, sages need virtually no care, except that purple, tricolor, and golden sage benefit from a winter mulch in the northern parts of their hardiness range.

Seed is a propagation option for regular culinary sage and clary sage: Sow indoors in early spring and do not cover. Look for seedlings in one to three weeks at 70°F. Set out transplants about 18 inches apart after the last frost date. Summer cuttings are another option for propagating culinary sage and its selections, as well as pineapple sage and Mexican bush sage. Layering in spring or fall is yet another effective technique for propagating the various varieties of culinary sage.

How to use them. Tall sages look good toward the back of a bed or border. Culinary sages work well at the front to middle of a planting; they also make interesting low hedges. Sages are great in containers, too. Pineapple sage is particularly good for a deck or patio planting, where you can easily reach the foliage and brush it to release the fragrance. The kitchen garden is another obvious place for culinary sages and pineapple sage.

What to plant with them. Try pairing gray-green culinary sage with either silvers — such as artemisias — or dark greens, such as parsley or rosemary. Purple sage also looks great with silver foliage and with yellow, pink, or red flowers. Try it with a mixed collection of yarrows. Golden sage pairs well with purple sage for an interesting color contrast; it's also an effective match with golden feverfew. Try 'Tricolor' with pink or white flowers, or with purple or dark green foliage.

Clary sage makes a good partner for a variety of purple-blue or white blooms. Combine pineapple sage with large, bright blooms, such as red petunias. And pair Mexican bush sage with other late-blooming flowers, such as dahlias (*Dahlia* species) or garden mums (*Dendranthema* × *morifolium*), and shrubs with showy berries or fall color, such as purple beautyberries (*Callicarpa* species) or burning bush (*Euonymus alata*).

SANTOLINAS

Known as: Lavender cotton *(Santolina chamaecyparissus,* also sold as *S. incana),* green santolina *(S. virens)*

Plant type: Perennial

Shrubby santolinas are best known for their aromatic silver or green foliage, but they also offer an eye-catching flower show in summer.

What they look like. Santolinas produce bushy mounds of green or silver-gray, ever-

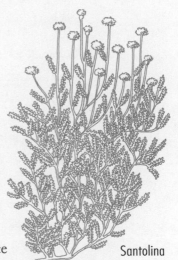

Santolina

green foliage. The foliage is definitely quite aromatic when you brush or rub it. Bright yellow, buttonlike flowers usually bloom in early or mid- to late summer. Height and spread vary from 1 to 2 feet, depending on how much you prune the fast-growing clumps.

Which one to choose. The species you're most likely to run across is lavender cotton *(Santolina chamaecyparissus,* also sold as *S. incana).*

The finely cut, gray-green, aromatic leaves are packed tightly on many-branched stems, and the flowers are bright golden yellow. Dwarf lavender cotton *(S. chamaecyparissus* var. *nana)* is more compact, up to about 1 foot tall. Green santolina *(S. virens)* has a similar, mounded habit but with narrow, bright green, aromatic foliage and yellow flowers.

Santolinas generally grow best in Zones 6 and 7, since they hate hot, humid summers and damp winters. You may have good luck with them in dry climates south of Zone 7, and they can also survive north of Zone 6 with excellent drainage and a winter mulch, such as conifer branches.

Where to plant them. Santolinas demand full sun and average, well-drained soil. Soggy soil is fatal, especially in winter, since santolinas' roots may rot.

How to grow them. Once you see new growth emerging in spring, remove any dead growth and trim the remaining stems back by one-half to two-thirds to shape the plant. Shearing again after bloom will remove the discolored old blooms and encourage bushier growth.

I've never had luck growing santolinas from seed, but I've heard that the trick is to sow about ⅛ inch deep in late winter and then chill the pots in the refrigerator for two to three months. Seedlings should appear in two to three weeks at 70°F. Taking cuttings in mid- to late summer and layering (see page 147) in spring or fall have been much more successful for me.

How to use them. Try santolinas as midborder accents or as ground covers on sunny, dry slopes for both floral and foliage interest. These plants tolerate regular trimming, so they also work well as a low clipped hedge or edging. They grow well in containers, too. Save trimmings for use in herbal wreaths.

What to plant with them. Lavender cotton's lacy, silver foliage looks great with both plain culinary sage and its various colored-leaf selections. Try green santolina with its silver sibling or with artemisias. All santolinas also pair well with rosemary and thymes, since they appreciate the same growing conditions.

SORRELS

Known as: Garden sorrel, dock, dock sorrel
(Rumex acetosa), French sorrel *(R. scutatus),*
bloody dock *(R. sanguineus)*

Plant type: Perennial

Sorrels certainly aren't high on the list of
fabulous flowering herbs, but the foliage of some
selections is worth a second look. The leaves of
some varieties have culinary uses, too.

Sorrel

What they look like. Sorrels grow in bushy clumps or mounds of
lanky, long-stalked, arrow-shaped leaves. In summer, slim stalks
arise from the clump, bearing slender, loose spikes of insignificant
small, reddish brown flowers.

Which one to choose. The two species you're most likely to find in
nurseries and catalogs are garden sorrel *(Rumex acetosa)* and French
sorrel *(R. scutatus).* Garden sorrel (sometimes also called French sorrel) has large, broad, thick, bright green leaves in upright clumps
usually 12 to 18 inches tall. Typical French sorrel is more compact (to
about 1 foot), with a more mat-forming habit and roughly spear-
shaped foliage. 'Silver Shield' is a very handsome selection of French
sorrel with silvery green leaves. My favorite sorrel is a species known
as bloody dock *(R. sanguineus).* This one produces clumps of narrow,
bright green leaves with bright red veins — a real eye-catcher in a
border! All of these sorrels should be hardy in Zones 5 to 9.

Another interesting sorrel is *R. flexuosus* — the whole plant is a
coppery brown, from the leaves to the tips of the flower stems. This
one is usually hardy south of Zone 6 but makes an interesting potted
plant in cooler climates if you bring it indoors in winter. Both
bloody dock and *R. flexuosus* can be tricky to find; look for them in
specialty mail-order catalogs or seed exchange seed lists.

Where to plant them. Sorrels can adapt to sun or partial shade, but
they seem to appreciate a steady supply of moisture (particularly for
garden sorrel).

How to grow them. Deadheading is a must, because sorrels can self-sow freely if left to their own devices. Leave one or two flower stems to mature if you would like just a few new plants; otherwise, pinch or cut off the flower stems as they emerge. A compost mulch will help keep the soil rich and moist. Divide plants every three or four years to keep them vigorous.

For propagation, it's easy to divide clumps in spring or fall. You can also sow seed ¼ inch deep indoors or outdoors in early to mid-spring. Look for seedlings in about a week at 70°F. Thin seedlings or set plants to stand about 1 foot apart.

How to use them. Enjoy sorrels as foliage accents in beds, borders, cottage gardens, and containers. The tangy leaves of garden and French sorrel also make them popular additions to kitchen gardens.

What to plant with them. Partner garden and French sorrels with colorful flowers or fine-textured foliage, such as calendulas and dill. Bloody dock pairs beautifully with bright red flowers, such as red petunias and red flowering tobacco (*Nicotiana alata* 'Domino Red'). *R. flexuosus* combines well with orange flowers, such as marigolds, and yellow-leaved plants, such as golden oregano.

SWEET WOODRUFF

Known as: Woodruff *(Galium odoratum)*

Plant type: Perennial

Sweet woodruff is one of the few herbs that really prefer shade, so it's an excellent candidate for mature landscapes. Its fast growth habit also makes it a great choice as a ground cover.

Sweet woodruff

What it looks like. This perennial herb grows in low, creeping carpets of brittle stems that bear whorls of small, slender, pointed leaves along their length. The leaves are bright, glossy green when young and age to dark green. In mid- to late spring, loose clusters of tiny white flowers bloom at the tips of the stems. The flowers have a light scent, but the name "sweet" really comes from the fragrance of the dried foliage — something like freshly cut hay with vanilla overtones. Sweet woodruff carpets grow 6 to 8 inches tall in leaf and up to 1 foot in bloom. It is usually hardy in Zones 5 to 9 but dislikes hot, humid summers.

Which one to choose. So far, there don't seem to be any selections of sweet woodruff. I've heard rumors of a pink-flowered form but haven't found a source for it.

Where to plant it. Give sweet woodruff a site in partial to full shade. It tolerates dry spells once established (and average to dry conditions do help control the spread), but it prefers evenly moist, well-drained soil.

How to grow it. In humid conditions, sweet woodruff benefits from a summer shearing, especially if you notice some black areas on the leaves. Shearing as soon as the flowers start to fade will also help prevent self-sowing. Use a string trimmer or grass shears to trim the top growth to about an inch above the ground (avoid cutting into the emerging new growth). Rake off the trimmings and toss them on your compost pile or dry them for potpourri.

Sweet woodruff seed germinates slowly, so it's easiest to start a patch from purchased plants. After that, divide established clumps in spring or fall as needed for propagation. Set plants 8 to 12 inches apart (use the closer spacing for quicker cover).

How to use it. Enjoy sweet woodruff as a ground cover in a woodland garden or under trees and shrubs. (It can't tolerate foot traffic, so make sure you add stepping-stones if you need access into the area.) Sweet woodruff also works well in pots or hanging baskets, if placed in shady spots.

What to plant with it. This pretty herb looks delicate, but it's a vigorous spreader, so it needs equally sturdy companions. Try it around large hostas; it looks particularly nice with those that have white-striped or golden foliage, such as 'Patriot' and 'Sum and Substance'. I also like sweet woodruff with variegated mints, such as pineapple mint.

THYMES

Known as: English thyme *(Thymus vulgaris)*, lemon thyme *(T. × citriodorus)*, silver thyme *(T. × citriodorus* 'Argenteus'), creeping or moss thyme *(T. praecox* ssp. *arcticus)*, woolly thyme *(T. praecox* ssp. *arcticus* 'Lanuginosus'), caraway thyme *(T. herba-barona)*

Plant type: Perennial

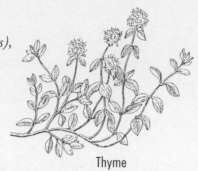

Thyme

Who can ever have too much thyme? These classic herbs, indispensable in the kitchen, may be small in stature, but they are big on charm — and of course, on fragrance!

What they look like. Thymes share their square stems and aromatic, opposite leaves with many other members of the mint family. These low-growing perennials produce clumps or carpets of thin, stiff, woody stems growing anywhere from 1 to 12 inches tall. The small, oval to pointed leaves attach directly to the stems or by very short stalks. The stems are stiff and woody and leaves are small, oval, and green, gray-green, or yellow-green in color. Tiny white, lilac, or pink flowers bloom in small clusters at the stem tips in early to midsummer.

Which one to choose. There are so many thymes to choose from, in a wide array of habits, scents, and leaf and flower colors, that it can be a challenge to decide where to begin your collection. I've described a few of the most popular thymes below, but they're just the beginning. Check out specialty growers' mail-order catalogs for the more unusual ones. Keep in mind that thyme nomenclature is somewhat confused, so you may see the same selection listed under different species in different catalogs.

Lemon thyme *(T. × citriodorus)* is another bushy type, with purplish pink flowers and tiny, bright green leaves that have an intense lemon scent. Variegated lemon thyme *(T. × citriodorus* 'Aureus') has a bright yellow edge around each leaf. Silver thyme *(T. × citriodorus*

'Argenteus') produces pink flowers and grayish green leaves, each with a silver-white edge. While commonly listed as a selection of lemon thyme, this one has more of a warm, spicy aroma, similar to English thyme. All of these should be hardy in Zones 5 to 9.

If you're looking for a low, spreading species, try creeping or moss thyme *(T. praecox* subspecies *arcticus)*. While its tiny, light green leaves aren't especially fragrant, it's worth growing for its 2-inch-tall sheets of tiny but bright blooms in early summer. 'Albus' has white flowers; 'Coccineus' produces bright reddish purple blooms. Woolly thyme (*Thymus praecox* subspecies *arcticus* 'Lanuginosus') is another mat-former, with tiny, gray-green, woolly leaves and pale pink flowers. Caraway thyme *(T. herba-barona)* is my favorite in the creeping category, with minute, dark green, caraway-scented leaves and pink to purplish flowers. These low-growing species and selections are generally hardy in Zones 4 to 9.

Where to plant them. Thymes demand full sun, but they do appreciate a bit of midday shade in the deep South. Light, well-drained soil is a must in any climate; thymes cannot tolerate soggy soil.

How to grow them. In spring, shear off the dead tips of bushy thymes back to emerging new growth. Bushy thymes can sprawl or die out in the center after several years, so trim them down to about 6 inches above the ground every two to three years. If the centers remain bare, divide the clumps and replant the vigorous outer portions. Bushy thymes may benefit from a loose mulch, such as conifer branches, in the northernmost parts of their range.

It's possible to grow species thymes from seed, but you'll get much faster and more uniform results by starting with purchased plants. Set plants 8 to 12 inches apart. For propagation, divide in spring, take cuttings in late spring to early summer, or layer in spring or fall.

How to use them. Thymes are invaluable in a variety of situations. The bushy species make excellent edgings for beds, borders, and pathways. Try low-growing thymes in the cracks in stone walls, between pavers or stepping-stones, or as ground covers on sunny slopes. Thymes grow well in containers, too.

What to plant with them. Pair thymes with other sun-loving plants that have broad or succulent leaves, such as hens-and-chicks (*Sempervivum* species) and sages, for a textural contrast. The green-leaved thymes look especially good with silvery foliage, such as that of artemisias, lavenders, and santolinas.

YARROWS

Known as: Common yarrow *(Achillea millefolium)*, woolly yarrow *(A. tomentosa)*

Plant type: Perennial

The bright flower clusters of these dependable perennial herbs are a welcome sight in any herbal landscape. They come in a rainbow of bright and pastel colors to fit into almost any sunny garden.

What they look like. Yarrows grow in clumps of deeply cut, green to grayish, aromatic foliage. Through summer, the plants send up slender stems topped with flattened, branching clusters of tiny flowers in a range of colors.

Yarrow

Which one to choose. In many areas of the country, you can see white-flowered *Achillea millefolium* growing wild along the roadsides. This spreading perennial is a little too vigorous for most gardens, but its cultivars and hybrids do have a place in the landscape. 'Cerise Queen' is a popular selection with bright green, feathery foliage and pink blooms on 2-foot stems. This cultivar is usually grown from seed, so the pink can vary widely from the preferred bright reddish pink to a rather washed-out pink. 'Summer Pastels Mix' is a seed strain that looks much like other *A. millefolium* selections but blooms in a range of soft yellow, pink, and orange hues. These are generally hardy in Zones 3 to 8.

Of course, when you think of yarrow, yellow flowers usually come to mind. 'Coronation Gold' is a classic hybrid with wide, golden yellow flower heads on stiff, 3-foot stems from early summer into early fall. Its deeply cut, gray-green foliage is also attractive. Try growing it in Zones 3 to 9. If you prefer a softer yellow, try the more compact 'Moonshine' (to 2 feet) or 'Anthea' (to 18 inches), both with gray-green foliage and light yellow flower heads. Both of these are generally hardy in Zones 4 to 8.

A. millefolium is also a parent of many exciting hybrids in a range of great colors. The bloom clusters of 'Paprika' look like a solid, strong red from a distance, but up close, you can see that each small flower has a yellow center. 'Salmon Beauty' has salmon-pink flower heads that fade to buff. Both of these grow to about 2 feet and are hardy in Zones 3 to 9. 'Fireland' blooms in a bright red that ages to salmon and then soft apricot-yellow, while 'Terra Cotta' has rusty orange flowers that fade to a pale orange-yellow. Both of these 2-foot cultivars have gray-tinted foliage and should be hardy in Zones 3 to 9.

Of course, when you think of yarrow, yellow flowers usually come to mind. 'Coronation Gold' is a classic hybrid with wide, golden yellow flower heads on stiff, 3-foot stems from early summer into early fall. Its deeply cut, gray-green foliage is also attractive. Try growing it in Zones 3 to 9. If you prefer a softer yellow, try the more compact 'Moonshine' (to 2 feet) or 'Anthea' (to 18 inches), both with gray-green foliage and light yellow flower heads. Both of these are generally hardy in Zones 4 to 8.

Woolly yarrow *(A. tomentosa)* is much lower growing than most of its relatives, reaching to about 8 inches in flower and 2 to 4 inches in leaf. The gray-green, hairy foliage makes a handsome carpet under the early to midsummer clusters of yellow flowers. Woolly yarrow grows best in Zones 3 to 7; it hates hot, humid summers.

Where to plant them. Yarrows thrive in full sun and average to poor soil. Shade or overly rich soil will produce weak, floppy stems that need staking. Good drainage is critical; yarrows hate wet feet, especially in winter.

How to grow them. Deadheading can help extend the bloom season and keep plants tidy, as well as prevent self-sowing of the species.

Trim off spent flower heads just above a leaf, then cut the whole stalk off at the base of the plant when no new blooms form. Yarrows benefit from division every three or four years; discard the dead centers and replant the vigorous outer portions.

You can propagate species yarrows, such as *A. millefolium,* and seed strains from seed. Sow indoors or outdoors in early spring; do not cover. Look for seedlings in two to four weeks at 65°F. Thin seedlings or set transplants about 2 feet apart (8 to 12 inches apart for woolly yarrow). Division in spring or fall is the easiest way to propagate the hybrids and cultivars.

How to use them. Yarrows work equally well in formal and informal gardens. Enjoy them in the middle to back of beds, borders, and cottage gardens. Woolly yarrow makes a great ground cover for sunny, dry slopes.

What to plant with them. It might be easier to list plants that *wouldn't* look good with yarrows! The bright golden or reddish yarrows pair well with other eye-catching colors, such as a glowing red bee balm (*Monarda* 'Jacob Cline'), bright purple-blue clustered bellflower *(Campanula glomerata),* multicolored daylilies, or yellow mulleins. Yellow yarrow also looks great paired with the yellow-striped green leaves of porcupine grass (*Miscanthus sinensis* 'Strictus') and the tiny, yellow-centered white daisies of feverfew. Try the pastel yarrows with purple or silver foliage, such as purple barberry (*Berberis thunbergii* 'Rose Glow' is particularly nice with pink yarrows), lamb's-ears, or artemisias. Peachy pink 'Salmon Beauty' and pale yellow 'Anthea' and 'Moonshine' combine beautifully with pale blue bell-flowers, such as *Campanula persicifolia* 'Telham Beauty'.

CHAPTER 4

GROWING HERBS
Successfully

Growing a beautiful herbal landscape doesn't take a magical "green thumb" — just a basic knowledge of good gardening practices. It begins with choosing plants that are adapted to the growing conditions your property has to offer, so you'll start with herbs that are developed to perform well. Whether you plan to grow those herbs from seed or buy them as transplants, knowing a few tips on seed-sowing and smart shopping will help get them off to a good start. And with a bit of routine care — weeding, watering, fertilizing, and the like — your herbs will thrive. Enjoy their bounty of foliage and flowers right in the garden, or bring some indoors for fresh use or drying — the perfect way to extend your herbal enjoyment right through the winter!

INVESTIGATING YOUR SITE

You can start a garden in one of two ways: Choose a site and then select suitable plants, or decide which herbs you simply *must* have and then look for a site that meets their needs. Starting with the site first definitely has its advantages, especially for beginning gardeners. You can come up with a plant list, buy all the herbs at one time, and install the garden all at once.

On the other hand, if you buy a bunch of herbs before you know their needs, there's a good chance they won't all grow well together, and you might end up digging several new gardens in different spots. Then you'll need to grow or buy *more* herbs to fill out each site. That's not necessarily a drawback if you're looking for a reason to sow more seeds or go nursery hopping for more herbs. And you'll probably end up creating several different gardens anyway, since it's likely that you'll want to try herbs that need different growing conditions.

LIGHT LEVELS

Whether you look at the amount of light a plant needs or evaluate the amount of light your site has to offer, you need to understand the vocabulary that books, nurseries, and seed companies use to describe the requirements of various plants. Here are some general guidelines to keep in mind:

Full sun: At least 6 hours of direct sun each day

Partial sun: Less than 6 but more than 4 hours of direct sun per day

Partial or light shade: Less than 4 hours of direct sun, or filtered sunlight for most of the day (a situation known as dappled shade)

Full shade: No direct sunlight and limited dappled shade

While most herbs appreciate full sun, some tolerate or even prefer a bit of shade, especially in hot-summer climates. To learn about the light preferences of particular herbs, check out the individual entries in Essential Landscape Herbs A to Z, starting on page 69. Seed packets, catalog descriptions, and in-the-pot labels are other good sources of this information.

Be Cautiously Adventurous

If you don't have the perfect growing conditions but simply *must* have a particular herb, buy just one and see how it does before you plan a garden around it. Some herbs that prefer sun, such as southernwood, can actually take some shade, although they'll produce more sprawling stems as a result. (In this case, shearing in late spring or early summer can encourage bushier growth.) Mints and other shade-loving herbs can also adapt to sunnier sites, but steady soil moisture is a must. Once you get the main part of your garden established, have fun experimenting with herbs in different conditions — you may be surprised at what you can get away with!

Keep in mind that light levels can vary dramatically over the course of a growing season. A site that is in full sun in April and May can be in deep shade by midsummer, when overhanging deciduous trees have leafed out fully. If you've just moved into a new home and don't know the sun and shade patterns around it, it's best to observe your site for one full growing season before you start planting. But if you don't have that much self-control, start out with only annual flowers and herbs the first year. You'll have *something* to look at while you're learning about the property, and you won't have wasted money on perennials that might not be right for your site.

SOIL MATTERS

The site's soil conditions also play an important role in determining which herbs you can grow. Herbs as a group have gotten a reputation for liking rocky, dry, infertile soil, and it's true that some herbs can tolerate those conditions remarkably well. But many herbs do just fine in what's called "ordinary garden soil." If other common plants are already growing in your garden, herbs should do fine there, too. If you suspect your soil might be less than ideal, however, see the following page for some clues to look for.

Water puddles stay on the site for more than 6 hours after rain or irrigation. This could indicate a drainage problem due to soil that is too compact or high in clay. Loosening the soil to a depth of 12 to 18 inches and working in generous amounts of compost or other organic matter before planting can help both problems. Or build raised beds framed with rocks, boards, or landscape timbers and fill them with garden soil that drains well. If you don't have good garden soil, you can purchase topsoil from garden centers and landscape contractors. Herbs thrive in raised beds!

Plants wilt frequently or the soil feels loose and sandy. Don't despair if you have dry, sandy soil; many herb gardeners will be envious. Plan your plantings around herbs that appreciate these conditions, such as lavenders, oreganos, santolinas, and thymes. Help out herbs that need more moisture by working a few handfuls of compost into their individual planting holes. Or prepare a separate planting site for them by digging a 3-inch layer of rich compost into the top 8 to 10 inches of soil. Mulching and regular watering during dry spells will also help herbs thrive in sandy sites.

Plants show poor growth. If the plants already on the site just aren't looking lush and healthy, your soil might have a nutrient imbalance. In that case, purchase a soil test kit from your local garden center or Cooperative Extension Service office, have a soil sample analyzed, and follow the suggestions on the report to fix any imbalances.

GETTING STARTED

Depending on your time, budget, and needs, you might decide to grow your herbs from seed or buy them as transplants. In this section, you'll find pointers for both approaches.

GROWING HERBS FROM SEED

Starting herbs from seed is fun and rewarding, and it's a great way to get quite a few plants for not much money. Annual herbs, including nasturtiums, basils, calendulas, dill, German chamomile, and nasturtiums, are good candidates for seed starting. A number of

Climate Considerations

Just like other annuals and perennials, herbs differ in the climate conditions they prefer. Hardiness zones are a good place to start, but they'll tell you only about the cold tolerance of an herb, and even that can vary widely depending on local conditions. For instance, I have trouble overwintering lavenders outdoors in my mid–Zone 6 garden, while a friend in Zone 4 has no trouble with them, probably due to her loose, sandy soil and dependable winter snow cover. (Snow insulates the ground, preventing rapid temperature changes, and protects plants from drying winter winds.)

Of course, cold tolerance is only part of the story: Heat and humidity tolerance is important, too. Many herbs thrive in *dry* heat, such as that of their Mediterranean homeland. These include herbs such as lavenders, rosemary, and thymes. If you live in a humid-summer climate, you might want to avoid large-scale or ground cover plantings of these herbs, since they'll be prone to rot. You might even decide to treat them as annuals and buy new plants each year.

Herbs with silvery foliage, including artemisias and santolinas, seem especially intolerant of sultry summers (and wet winters as well).

perennial herbs also give good results from seed. These include anise hyssop, Roman chamomile, chives, fennel, hyssop, English lavender, lemon balm, parsley, and culinary sage.

Sowing seed outdoors. It can't get much easier than this! Simply loosen the soil and then smooth the surface with a rake to create a level seedbed. Check the seed packet for suggested sowing times, as well as depth and spacing guidelines. When you are ready to plant, scatter the seed as evenly as possible over the soil surface. If you need to cover the seed, rake the area lightly or scatter some loose soil over the surface; otherwise, gently press the seed into the soil with your fingers. Water the area, being careful not to wash away the seed, and keep it evenly moist until sprouts appear. Thin the seedlings to the spacing suggested on the packet, and you've got your herbs growing.

Sowing seed indoors. Some seeds, such as those of basils, need more warmth than typical outdoor conditions can provide. Other herbs, including hyssop and lavender, tend to grow slowly, so they appreciate the controlled conditions indoor sowing can provide.

Gather some sterile seed-starting mix (available at your local garden center) and some clean, 3- to 4-inch plastic pots or six-packs. (You may have lots of these in your garage from previous purchases of annuals.) Place the mix in a bowl or bucket, add some warm water, and knead the mix with your hands. You want the mix to be evenly damp but not soggy; add more water or dry mix as needed. Fill the containers with the moistened seed-starting mix and then sow the seeds according to the depth and spacing suggested on the packet.

Place sown pots on a warm windowsill with bright but indirect light — or better yet, under a shop-light fixture filled with fluorescent bulbs. Set your lights on a timer so they're on for 14 to 16 hours a day.

Shop lights are great for indoor seed-starting projects. Hang them from chains so they're about 2 inches above your seed pots at first; raise them as the seedlings grow.

Check the pots at least once a day. If the surface of the mix is drying out, spray it with a mist of warm water or set the whole pot in a tray holding an inch or two of warm water until the surface appears moist.

As your seedlings appear, reduce watering slightly so the surface of the mix dries out a bit between waterings. Thin the seedlings as recommended on the packet, transplanting them to individual pots if needed. Use scissors to snip off unwanted seedlings; pulling them out can damage the roots of remaining plants.

BUYING HERBS

Starting a garden with purchased herbs isn't just the quick-and-easy way — it's sometimes the *only* way to get the herbs you need. French tarragon, for instance, rarely produces seed, so it is propagated "vegetatively," mainly by cuttings or division. Vegetative propagation is also a must for reproducing cultivars of many other herbs, such as 'Marshall's Delight' bee balm and 'Moonshine' yarrow. So if you are looking for a specific leaf or flower color, or if you need only one or two plants of a particular herb, buying started plants just makes sense.

Hardening Off

If you grow your own herbs from seed or buy greenhouse-grown transplants, keep in mind that they are used to warm, humid, wind-free conditions. To help them adapt to the great outdoors, you'll need to expose them to those harsher conditions gradually. This process is called hardening off.

About a week before you are ready to move your herbs to the garden, set them outside in a sheltered spot, such as on a covered porch or next to a bushy shrub. Leave them out for an hour or two the first day, gradually extending the time and increasing the amount of light until they can be out for a full day and night before planting.

Potted seedlings can dry out quickly, so check them often and water them once or twice a day, as needed.

When shopping for any herb, look for displays that are clean and well maintained. Avoid pots that are weedy or wilted. (Yes, watering can perk up wilted herbs, but their growth will be stunted if they've been allowed to wilt frequently.) And, of course, don't buy herbs with obvious pest or disease problems. Inspect all parts of the plants carefully, including the bases of the stems and the undersides of the leaves. If you see pests or signs of other problems, such as chewed leaves, speckled or discolored foliage, or wilted or distorted growth, put that plant back — and consider shopping elsewhere!

KEEPING HERBS HAPPY

As a group, herbs are fairly low maintenance, but they do appreciate the same general care you'd give to any other garden plant. Here are some pointers to help keep your herbs looking their best.

WATERING

If you've chosen herbs that are suited to the site you've put them in, they shouldn't need much special attention to watering, especially once they are established. Right after planting, though, it's a good idea to keep the soil evenly moist (though not soggy) to make sure the limited root systems can reach the water they need. Watering thoroughly every week or two (if rain is lacking) during the first growing season will get your herbs off to a great start.

Once herbs are established in the conditions they prefer, they should need watering only during dry spells, especially if you've covered the soil with mulch. It's smart to plan ahead, though, by installing soaker hoses in your gardens in spring. Snake them through the planting to evenly distribute the water, cover them with a layer of mulch, and you'll be all ready to water if needed later in the season. Besides delivering water right where it's

Pay special attention to watering during your herbs' first growing season.

needed, soaker hoses help keep plant leaves dry, discouraging disease problems. It's easiest to lay soaker hoses as the plants are just emerging, but if you need to do it later, just weave them carefully around the plants. It's handy to have a helper for this job.

Soaker hoses are made of a porous material that allows moisture to seep out all along their length. The water comes out slowly, so it soaks into the soil and gets right to the roots, where it's needed!

MULCHING

Mulches serve many purposes, so mulch management is perhaps the most important part of caring for any garden. Mulch will help to keep the soil from drying out by minimizing evaporation, so it reduces watering chores. It also shades the soil, discouraging weed seeds from sprouting and moderating soil temperatures around the roots. As they break down, organic mulches add a small but steady supply of nutrients to the soil. A well-chosen mulch can also make a beautiful background for your handsome herbs.

If you use an organic mulch, apply a 1- to 2-inch layer immediately after planting. Leave a 2- to 4-inch-diameter mulch-free ring around the base of each plant. Mulch piled against the stems can hold excess moisture there and promote rot. Each year, add more mulch in spring if needed to maintain that 1- to 2-inch layer. In hot-summer areas, you may need to add more mulch in summer, too, to keep the layer at the right level.

FEEDING

While many herbs can adapt to less than ideal fertility, most thrive in soil that can provide a steady, balanced supply of nutrients. Fertilizing starts at planting time. Taking a soil test is a great way to find out exactly what nutrients are in your soil, and in what balance.

Mulch Materials

Which mulch is best? There is no one answer! It depends in great part on what is readily available at a reasonable price in your area. In the Southeast, for example, pine needles may be a good choice, while cocoa bean shells are an aromatic option if you happen to live near a chocolate factory. Here's some information on a few widely available options; check with other gardeners in your area to learn about locally available mulch materials.

MULCH MATERIAL	MULCH THICKNESS	COMMENTS
Chopped leaves	2 to 3 inches	Usually free for the asking, the windfall of autumn leaves provides ample material for mulching. Whole leaves can smother some plants, though, so it's best to shred them first. If you don't have a leaf shredder, try using a bagging mower. Chopped leaves break down quickly, so you might need to remulch several times during the year.
Compost	2 to 3 inches	Commercial or homemade compost offers many benefits. It's usually inexpensive or free, it's an attractive dark color, and it's a good source of nutrients and organic matter. On the downside, I find that fine-textured compost can dry out quickly and crust over, making it hard to rewet; avoid this problem by using not-quite-finished (still a bit lumpy) compost for mulching.
Shredded bark or wood chips	1 to 2 inches	These materials are long lasting and good at suppressing weeds. One drawback is that they may draw nitrogen out of the soil as they decompose, so it's smart to apply them over a ½-inch layer of compost.
Gravel	1 to 2 inches	Available in a range of sizes, shapes, and colors, gravels make excellent mulches in humid-summer climates. Also try them around lavenders, thymes, and other herbs that need excellent drainage if you live where winters are wet.

You can get soil test kits from your local Cooperative Extension Service office or from many garden centers. Follow the directions in the package for collecting samples and interpreting the fertilizer recommendations you get back. Working compost into the soil at planting time will also add a small amount of nutrients into the soil, as well as build your soil's organic matter content.

After that, the fertilizing routine depends on the herbs you are growing. Mediterranean herbs, such as lavenders, oreganos, rosemary, and santolinas, will get by just fine on a light layer of compost each year or two. A 2-inch layer of compost or a scattering of all-purpose organic fertilizer added to the soil each spring will meet the needs of most other herbs. A few heavy feeders, including basils, mints, bee balms, and basils, appreciate a little extra compost or fertilizer, or a dose of fish emulsion or other liquid organic fertilizer, in early to midsummer. (If you're trying to minimize the spread of your bee balm or mint, skip this extra feeding!)

Mulching in Warm, Humid Regions

A word of caution for gardeners in warm, humid regions: While organic mulches can work magic in most areas, you need to manage them carefully in moist climates. Besides keeping the soil too wet, they can provide a haven for slugs and snails. Mulching with coarse sand or gravel instead of organic material will help keep your herbs dry.

WEEDING

Weeds compete with your garden plants for moisture, nutrients, and space, so it's important to keep these thugs under control. The same techniques you use around your vegetables and flowers will work for herbs, too: mulching to discourage weeds from sprouting and hand-pulling any weeds that do pop through. I make it a rule that I must pull any weed as soon as I spot it. It's much too easy to forget to go back the next day, and by the time you notice it again, it may have already dropped seed or crept several feet. Small weeds are easier to pull, anyway, especially when the soil is moist.

Controlling Spreading Herbs

Sometimes the problem isn't weeds *in* your herbs, it's that your herbs *are* the weeds! Left unchecked, bee balms, mints, sweet woodruff, and other creeping herbs can spread rapidly through underground root systems, crowding out less rowdy companions. Herbs that produce copious amounts of seed can also be a problem, leaving hundreds or thousands of offspring that appear in all parts of your landscape. Herbs that can self-sow prolifically include angelicas, anise hyssop, chives, dill, fennel, feverfew, lemon balm, mulleins, and sorrels.

Controlling herbs that spread by underground runners. Prevent spreading by giving herbs a site of their own, so they can creep at will without invading other plants. Plant them against a building or in an open or shady site where they can make an effective ground cover.

Another approach is to plant creeping herbs within some kind of barrier, so their roots are controlled. Pots are a great idea, but be sure to set them on a hard surface, so they don't root into the ground through the drainage holes! You can also dig a large hole and sink a bottomless 5-gallon bucket into it. Leave an inch or two of the rim above ground to discourage the spread of surface roots, and plant your spreader in the bucket. Check the herb every month or two to make sure it's not creeping over the barrier.

Herbs that spread by seed. Simply cut off the flowers before they form seed. If you do want to keep a few seedlings, then just leave one or two flowers.

Controlling herbs that are already out of control. If letting the aggressive herb keep that space isn't an option, you have a big job ahead of you. Dig out as much of it as you can find, getting as many of its roots as possible. Keep an eye on that spot over the next few months and immediately remove any shoots you see. I'd suggest waiting until the following fall or spring to make sure all the roots are gone before replanting that site with more-controlled choices.

DEALING WITH PESTS AND DISEASES

Good general care goes a long way to keeping your herbs naturally problem resistant. On occasion, though, you might spot a problem — perhaps an infestation of aphids on your nasturtiums, mildew on your bee balm, or sparse growth on your thymes. Handling these and other problems on herbs is just like protecting any other garden plants. First, determine what is causing the problem, and then carry out the appropriate plan of action. For instance, chewed foliage and discolored or stippled leaves are usually signs of pests, while leaf spots, dark, water-soaked stems, or a powdery gray coating on shoots and buds are all common disease symptoms.

Pest control. If you actually see the pests, squashing them with your fingers or rinsing them off the plants with water from a hose nozzle (being sure to spray both sides of the leaves) might do the trick. If you need more help, insecticidal soap sprays, available at your local garden center, will control a variety of garden pests. Just remember that these sprays can also harm beneficial insects, so use them only as directed on infested plants. And avoid using any sprays (other than water) on herbs you plan to eat!

Disease control. If your herbs are rotting at the base, you probably have a drainage problem; replant new herbs in a better-drained spot. If the problem continues, the herbs just might not be suited to your climate; either choose other herbs or buy new plants each year. If powdery mildew is a problem, try dividing or thinning out crowded clumps to improve air circulation around the leaves. Replacing the problem-prone plants with mildew-resistant cultivars is a great way to reduce the chances of this problem in following years.

GROOMING

Regular attention to trimming and to removing dead flowers is often the difference between a so-so garden and a great one. There's just something about a well-maintained garden that makes it looked loved. This kind of regular attention also helps keep your herbs healthy and vigorous.

Pruning. Spring is the time to clean up any remaining top growth (seed heads, dead leaves, and the like) that you didn't remove in the fall. It's also a good time to cut back woody-stemmed herbs, such as lavenders and thymes, to encourage bushy new growth. I like to wait until mid- or even late spring, so I can see what is dead and what is sprouting. Trim out all of the dead growth; then cut the remaining stems back by about half to shape the plant. Use a clean, sharp pair of pruning shears to trim individual plants or hedge trimmers to shear formal herbal hedges. To keep formal hedges neat, trim again as needed every two to three weeks until midsummer. (Avoid pruning after that, or your plants might produce lush new growth that can be damaged by early frosts.)

Deadheading. Removing faded flowers offers many benefits for just a few minutes' work. Besides making your herbs look better, it can encourage them to form fresh, leafy growth or more flowers. Deadheading also prevents angelicas, dills, fennel, feverfew, sorrels, and other self-sowing herbs from getting weedy.

If you're dealing with a plant that has large single flowers, such as bee balms and calendulas, simply pinch or snip them off just above the uppermost set of leaves or above an emerging flower bud. Lady's man-

Give 'em a Pinch!

Many bushy herbs respond well to a light pinching every week or two during the growing season. Depending on the plant, the benefit is either new leaf growth or fresh blooms. Pinching is especially important for best results on basils, since flower production can affect the flavor of the leaves. Simply pinch or clip the growing tip off the end of each shoot to prevent flower formation and promote leaf production.

Bringing Herbs Indoors

If you plan to bring rosemary, scented geraniums, and other tender herbs indoors for the winter, you need to start planning well before frost. Where space isn't a consideration, you can bring whole plants indoors. Here are three ways to do it:

- If window space is limited, consider taking cuttings of your favorite herbs in midsummer; that way, you'll have fairly small plants to deal with over the winter. (See Making More Herbs on page 144 for tips on how to take cuttings.) In spring, trim back any leggy growth, harden off the plants, and set them out in the garden after danger of frost.

- If your herbs are already growing in pots, just check them carefully for pests and diseases in early fall and treat any problems as needed while they are still outdoors.

- If your plants are growing in the garden, dig them up in early to mid-fall and plant them in pots with commercial potting mix. Water them well and set them in a shady place for a few days to recover from the shock of transplanting. Check them for pests and diseases and treat any problems before moving them indoors.

tles and yarrows produce their bloom clusters on stalks held above a leafy rosette; clip these stalks off at the base of the plant. On herbs that hold their flowers just above the foliage, such as lavenders, oreganos, santolinas, and thymes, a few snips with hedge trimmers make short work of deadheading. Catmint and lemon balm flowers are close to or among their foliage; cut the whole plants back by one-half to two-thirds, and they'll produce a flush of new growth and possibly more flowers.

Don't just toss your herb prunings on your compost pile; in many cases, they are still useful. Bring them indoors for drying or enjoy them fresh for cooking or craft projects, such as fragrant wreaths, bouquets, or potpourri.

PREPARING HERBS FOR WINTER

After midsummer, stop fertilizing and pruning herbs so their shoots will have time to adjust to the gradually cooling temperatures.

After the first frost, pull out blackened annual herb plants and add them to your compost pile. Some gardeners like to remove all dead top growth from their plants during fall cleanup, so the garden looks tidy during the winter. Others prefer to leave that job for spring, thinking that the stems add winter interest and provide food for birds and other wildlife. Either approach seems to work well; it just depends on your tastes.

Unless you live where you can count on winter-long snow cover, it's a good idea to protect your perennial herbs from drying winter winds and fluctuating temperatures. A few inches of chopped leaf mulch applied after the ground freezes will help keep the soil temperature constant. A layer of evergreen boughs can provide extra protection. Don't be in a hurry to apply these mulches; wait until the soil is frozen or you might provide a perfect home for voles, mice, and other pests that can damage your plants over the winter. Remove these mulches in spring as soon as temperatures moderate.

MAKING MORE HERBS

Learning how to propagate herbs is a wonderful way to expand your herbal landscape without spending a fortune. These three basic techniques — cuttings, division, and layering — are easy to learn and rewarding to use. And unlike seed-grown herbs, your new plants will be exact copies of their parents, a definite plus if you need more plants with a specific height, habit, or flower color, or, beyond considerations of garden design, if you want culinary herbs with the same flavor.

CUTTINGS

Taking cuttings allows you to produce dozens of new plants with minimal disturbance to the parent plant. This technique works great for a wide variety of herbs, including sages, mints, and scented geraniums, just to name a few!

When to take cuttings. I like to do most of my cuttings in midsummer, when shoots have firmed up a bit but before they get tough. (If shoots are too soft, they tend to wilt quickly; if they are hard, they root slowly.) But if you want to take cuttings at another time, it's worth a try; plants are amazingly forgiving.

How to take cuttings. Using a clean, sharp pair of scissors or pruning shears, snip off a shoot tip roughly 4 inches long. It should have at least two, preferably three or more, sets of leaves. Using your knife or clippers, remove the leaves from the lower one-half to two-thirds of the stem, then insert the bottom half of the stem into a pot of moist growing medium. I like to use a commercial seed-starting medium or a mixture of half vermiculite and half perlite. (Alternatively, dip the cut stem ends in rooting hormone, available at garden centers, before planting them.) Use a pencil or your fingers to firm the medium around the base of each cutting and then water thoroughly. Place the pot in a warm and humid spot that's bright, but out of direct sun. Water as needed to keep the soil evenly moist. In two to three weeks, you should notice new growth emerging. Wait another week or two before transplanting seedlings to individual pots, if desired.

A 4-inch pot can hold three or four herb cuttings. Once they root, move them to individual pots, or keep them as a group to get one bushy new plant quickly.

DIVISION

Multiplying perennial herbs by dividing them results in only a few new plants at a time, but you'll have already-rooted sections that are ready to go back in the garden right away. This technique works best on spreaders, such as bee balms and mints, and clump formers, such as lady's mantle, catmints, and lemon balm. Rosette-forming herbs such as angelicas and mulleins generally don't respond well to division; use seeds for these instead.

Make a Miniature Greenhouse

Many cuttings root best in humid conditions, such as those in a green-house. Fortunately, you can reproduce those conditions on a smaller scale by placing pots of cuttings in a clear plastic sweater box or by enclosing individual pots in clear plastic bags. Set these enclosures in a warm bright place out of direct sunlight, and you might be amazed at the great results. A word of warning, though: I find this technique doesn't work well with herbs that prefer dry conditions, such as artemisias, lavenders, rosemary, and santolinas.

When to divide herbs. The ideal times for division are early spring, just as new growth is emerging, and early fall, as the leaves are beginning to die down.

How to divide herbs. Dig deeply around all sides of the plant and lift the clump from the soil. Use your fingers or a fork or trowel to separate the rootball into sections. You can make three or four good-sized divisions — with multiple shoots and roots — from a clump at least 6 inches in diameter. Smaller divisions are okay if you need more new plants, but just make sure each new section has at least one shoot and some roots. It's best to plant very small divisions in pots to help them bulk up before replanting. Large divisions — those with at least three shoots — can go back in the garden right away.

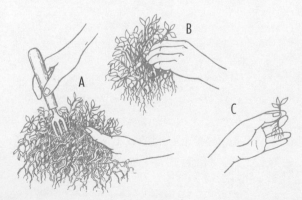

Dig up a clump of herbs and use a fork or your fingers to gently tease sections apart (A). You can take a small division with several plants (B), or even individual shoots (C).

LAYERING

As you're working among your herbs, you may notice that a stem has sprawled along the ground and taken root where it touched the soil. This is called layering, and it's a technique you can use to propagate a number of perennial herbs. It works especially well on those with woody but flexible stems, including southernwood, hyssop, lavenders, rosemary, sages, santolinas, and thymes.

When to layer herbs. You can use this technique any time the ground isn't frozen, though spring or summer are best, so that the new plants have time to get well established during the growing season.

How to layer herbs. To start a layer, carefully bend a shoot down to the ground. Loosen the soil in the area where the stem touched the earth and remove a few of the leaves from the stem at that spot. If you wish, you can lightly scratch the stem with a knife to help promote rooting. Bend the stem to the ground again and nestle it into the loosened soil, so the exposed section of stem is covered but the shoot tip is exposed. If needed, use a U-shaped piece of wire to hold the stem down. Water thoroughly and keep the area evenly moist.

Layers can take weeks or months to root. When you think the layer is rooted, try removing any covering and tugging on the shoot tip to see if it resists. If it is still not rooted, replace the covering. When the layer is well rooted, cut it away from the parent plant and move it to a pot or another spot in your garden.

I like to place a rock or brick over a finished layer. Besides holding the shoot down firmly, it helps keep the area moist, encouraging good root growth.

PUTTING IT ALL TOGETHER

In this chapter, I've covered just the basics you need to grow herbs successfully; it would be easy to write a whole book on the subject. Fortunately, herbs are very forgiving, so you don't need years of experience or a degree in horticulture to get the best from them. Give them a good site, mulch regularly, trim them up when you get a chance, and you'll enjoy a lovely herbal landscape for years to come!

Once you experience the fun of growing herbs, chances are you'll want to learn more about them. In the resources on page 149, I've listed some of my favorite herb magazines and books. Of course, it's also fun to find other gardeners who are equally passionate about your favorite hobby, so I've also given contact information for two national herb-related organizations. Check out local garden clubs, too; they're a great place to make new friends and to share plants and knowledge.

The choice of garden ornaments is practically endless, limited only by your personal taste and creativity. Just don't overdo it; one or two accents are interesting, but more than that can give your garden a cluttered look.

HERBAL
Resources

HERB ORGANIZATIONS

The Flower & Herb Exchange
3076 North Winn Road
Decorah, IA 52101
Phone: 319-382-5990
Fax: 319-382-5872
Annual flower and herb seed exchanges among members. A more limited list available to non-members.

The Herb Society of America, Inc.
9019 Kirtland Chardon Road
Kirtland, OH 44094
Phone: 440-256-0514
Fax: 440-256-0541
E-mail: herbs@herbsociety.org
Web site: www.herbsociety.org
Publications and a seed exchange available to members of this organization.

MAIL-ORDER SUPPLIERS

Catalog prices change from year to year. We suggest that you call, fax, or check the Web site before ordering from a catalog.

Caprilands Herb Farm
534 Silver Street
P.O. Box 190
Coventry, CT 06238
Phone: 860-742-7244
Web site: www.caprilands.com
Herbs, teas, potpourri, fragrance oils, and more.

Companion Plants
7247 N. Coolville Ridge Road
Athens, OH 45701
Phone: 740-592-4643
Fax: 740-593-3092
E-mail: complants@frognet.net
Web site: www.frognet.net
    /companion_plants
A wide variety of herb plants, including many unusual selections.

The Cook's Garden
P.O. Box 5010
Hodges, SC 29653-5010
Phone: 800-457-9703
Fax: 800-457-9705
E-mail: orders@cooksgarden.com
Web site: www.cooksgarden.com
A wonderful selection of vegetable and herb seeds.

Sandy Mush Herb Nursery
316 Surrett Cove Road
Leicester, NC 28748-2014
Phone: 828-683-5517
Fax: 828-683-2014
Great selection of herb plants and seeds.

Shepherd's Garden Seeds
30 Irene Street
Torrington, CT 06790-6658
Phone: 860-482-3638
Fax: 860-482-0532
E-mail: custsrv@shepherdseeds.com
Web site: www.shepherdseeds.com
Another excellent source for unusual herbs and vegetable seeds.

Southern Perennials & Herbs
98 Bridges Road
Tylertown, MS 39667-9339
Phone: 601-684-1769
Fax: 601-684-3729
E-mail: sph@neosoft.com
Web site: www.s-p-h.com

Well-Sweep Herb Farm
205 Mt. Bethel Road
Port Murray, NJ 07865
Phone: 908-852-5390
Fax: 908-852-1649
Common and unusual herb plants, and some seeds.

HERB PERIODICALS

The Herb Companion
Interweave Press
201 East Fourth Street
Loveland, CO 80537-5655
Phone: 800-456-6018
Fax: 970-667-8317
E-mail: HerbCompanion@hcpress.com
Web site: www.interweave.com/iwpsite/
   herbie/herbie.html

The Herb Quarterly
P.O. Box 689
San Anselmo, CA 94979
Phone: 800-371-HERB
Fax: 414-458-2955
E-mail: HerbQuart@aol.com
Web site: www.herbquarterly.com

HERB BOOKS

Brooklyn Botanic Garden. *Gardening for Fragrance*. New York: Brooklyn Botanic Garden, Inc., 1990. ISBN 0945352549. A wonderful collection of articles on growing all kinds of fragrant plants.

Kowalchik, Claire, and William H. Hylton, eds. *Rodale's Illustrated Encyclopedia of Herbs*. Emmaus, PA: Rodale Press, 1988. ISBN 087596964X. Detailed entries on individual herbs, with articles on many aspects of growing and using herbs.

McClure, Susan. *The Herb Gardener: A Guide for All Seasons*. Pownal, VT: Storey Communications, Inc., 1997. ISBN 0882668730. A comprehensive guide to growing and enjoying herbs.

Simmons, Adelma Grenier. *Herb Gardening in Five Seasons*. New York: Hawthorn Books, 1964, 1992. ISBN 0452266599. Insights on growing and using herbs, including great ideas for theme gardens.

Sombke, Laurence. *Beautiful Easy Herbs: How to Get the Most from Herbs — In Your Garden and in Your Home*. Emmaus, PA: Rodale Press, 1997. ISBN 087596771X. Overview of using herbs in gardening, cooking, and crafts.

ACKNOWLEDGMENTS

Many thanks to my two constant Sheltie companions — Guinevere (Bronwyn Pendragon CGC, TDI) and her mother, Granny (Ch. Bronwyn Babci CGC) — for allowing me a few hours of work time between dumbbell sessions, agility training, manners classes, obedience practice, and nursing-home visits. And special thanks to Mom and her two super-Shelties — Ouija (Am./Can. Ch. Haven House Bronwyn Hylite CGC) and daughter Alyssa (Ch. Bronwyn Felicity) — for coming to visit on weekends and entertaining my girls so I could have some uninterrupted writing time!

USDA Plant Hardiness Zone Map

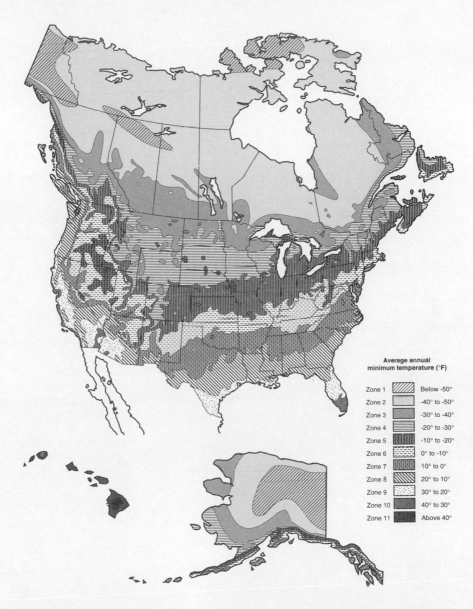

	Average annual minimum temperature (°F)
Zone 1	Below -50°
Zone 2	-40° to -50°
Zone 3	-30° to -40°
Zone 4	-20° to -30°
Zone 5	-10° to -20°
Zone 6	0° to -10°
Zone 7	10° to 0°
Zone 8	20° to 10°
Zone 9	30° to 20°
Zone 10	40° to 30°
Zone 11	Above 40°

This map was revised in 1990 and is recognized as the best indicator of minimum temperatures available. Look at the map to find your area, then match its color to the key at the right. When you've found your color, the key will tell you what hardiness zone you live in. Remember that the map is a general guide; your particular conditions may vary.

Index

Page references in *italics* indicate illustrations;
page references in **bold** indicate tables.